The Roman Empire had a powerful army that helped the empire become the strongest, most powerful, and most influential force in Europe, North Africa, and the Middle East for hundreds of years. Mostly they won, but sometimes they lost. Read about the great battles of the Roman legions!

Roman Power

The Roman Republic grew and expanded its power, and the Roman Empire that followed it became the greatest force of its time, because of the effectiveness of its armies and navies. Here are some of the great battles they fought, sometimes winning and sometimes not!

The Armies of Rome

Roman armies were organized into legions, highly-trained fighters who were usually better-equipped, better-fed, and had better generals than the armies they faced. Each legion had about 5,000 men.

The smallest unit in a legion was a "century" of between 50 and 80 men, with a centurion as its leader. The centuries were organized into larger groups as needed for battles. In the early days of the Republic those larger groups were called "maniples" and followed certain traditions that meant most legions fought with the maniples in three parallel lines. Later, the army was reorganized into cohorts of about 500 men each, which were stronger, better coordinated, and more adaptable to battlefield circumstances than the maniples had been.

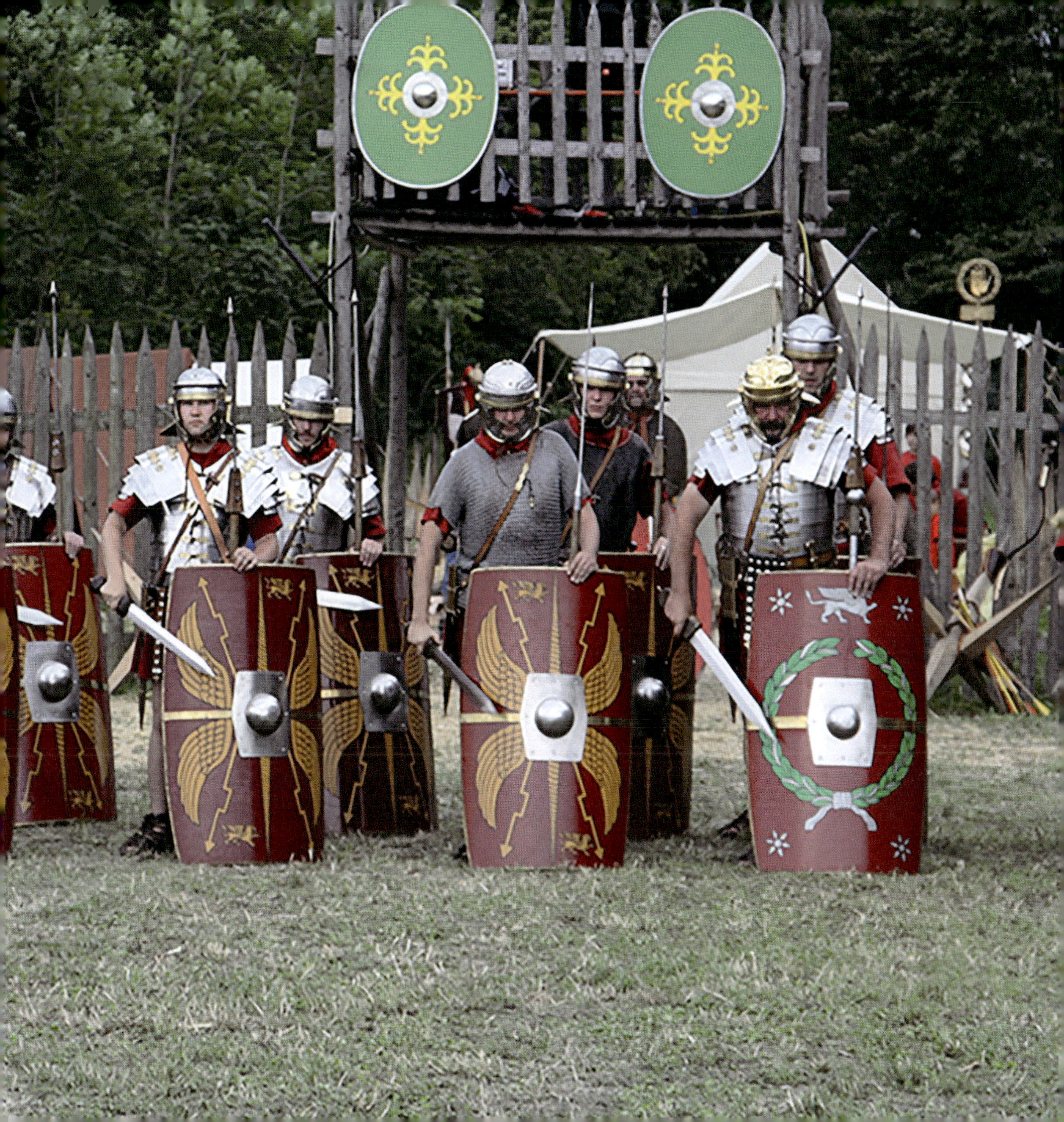

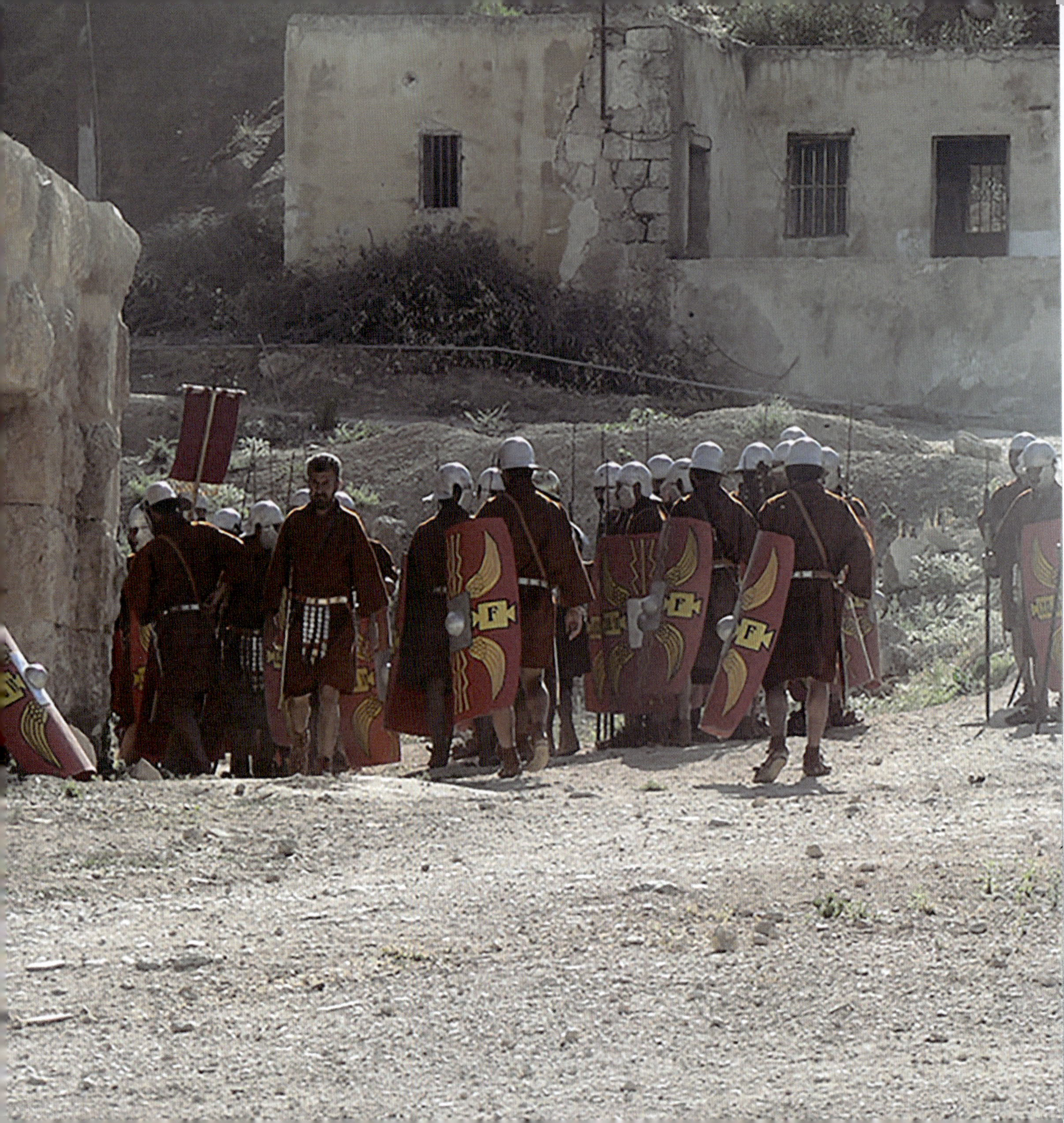

Each Roman legion had cavalry units, which scouted the land ahead and in battle protected the flanks of the legion when not attacking the enemy. However, the main force was always the foot soldiers.

On the battlefield each cohort occupied a space about 500 feet wide and fifty feet deep. The front row were the first people to fight whatever army faced them. After a few minutes the cohort commander would blow a whistle. All the fighters from the first row would shove their enemies back, take a step to the right, and let the second row step forward. Then the soldier from the first row would move to the back of the cohort to rest. They would move forward, whistle blast by whistle blast, until it was their turn to fight again.

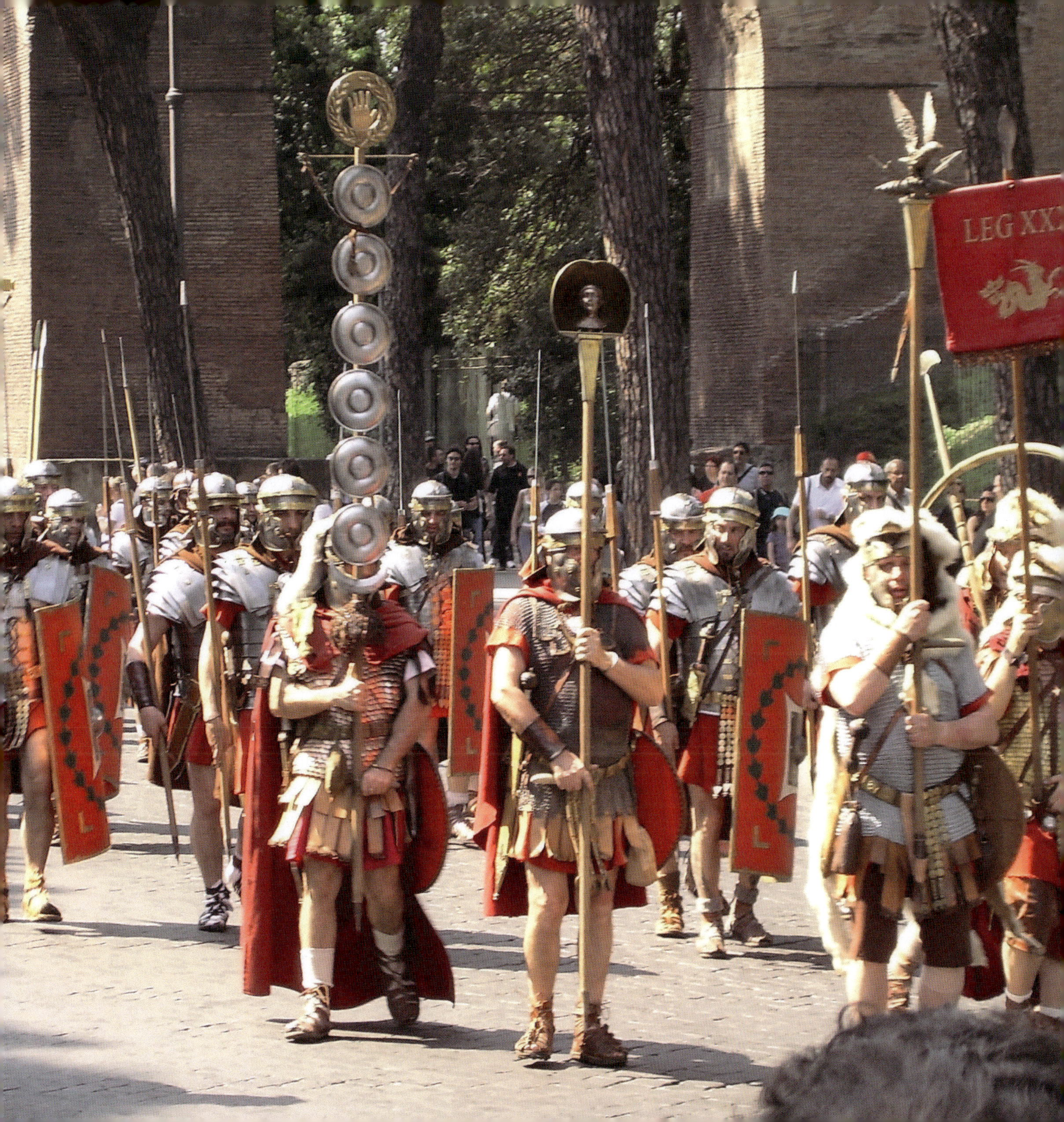
LEG XX

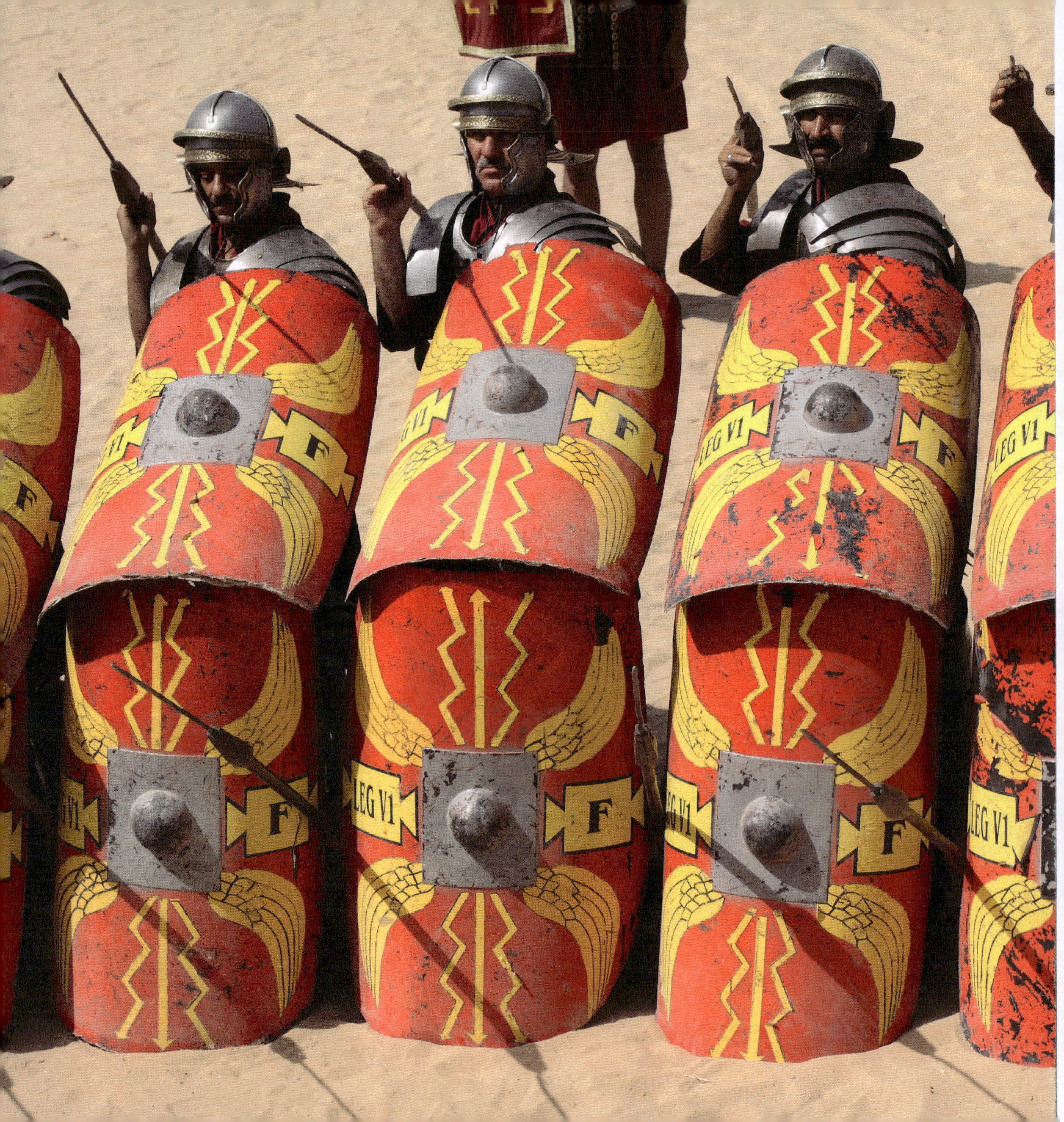
LEG V1
F

The success of the legions depended a lot on good generalship, and good communication of commands from the commanding general right down to the soldier waiting for the centurion's next whistle blast.

Great Battles

Siege of Syracuse (214-212 B.C.E.)

The Romans held half of Sicily and Carthage took over the other half. Rome decided to kick the Carthaginians off the island. They took advantage of a rebellion in the city of Syracuse by those who did not support Carthage, and attacked by sea and land to conquer the city.

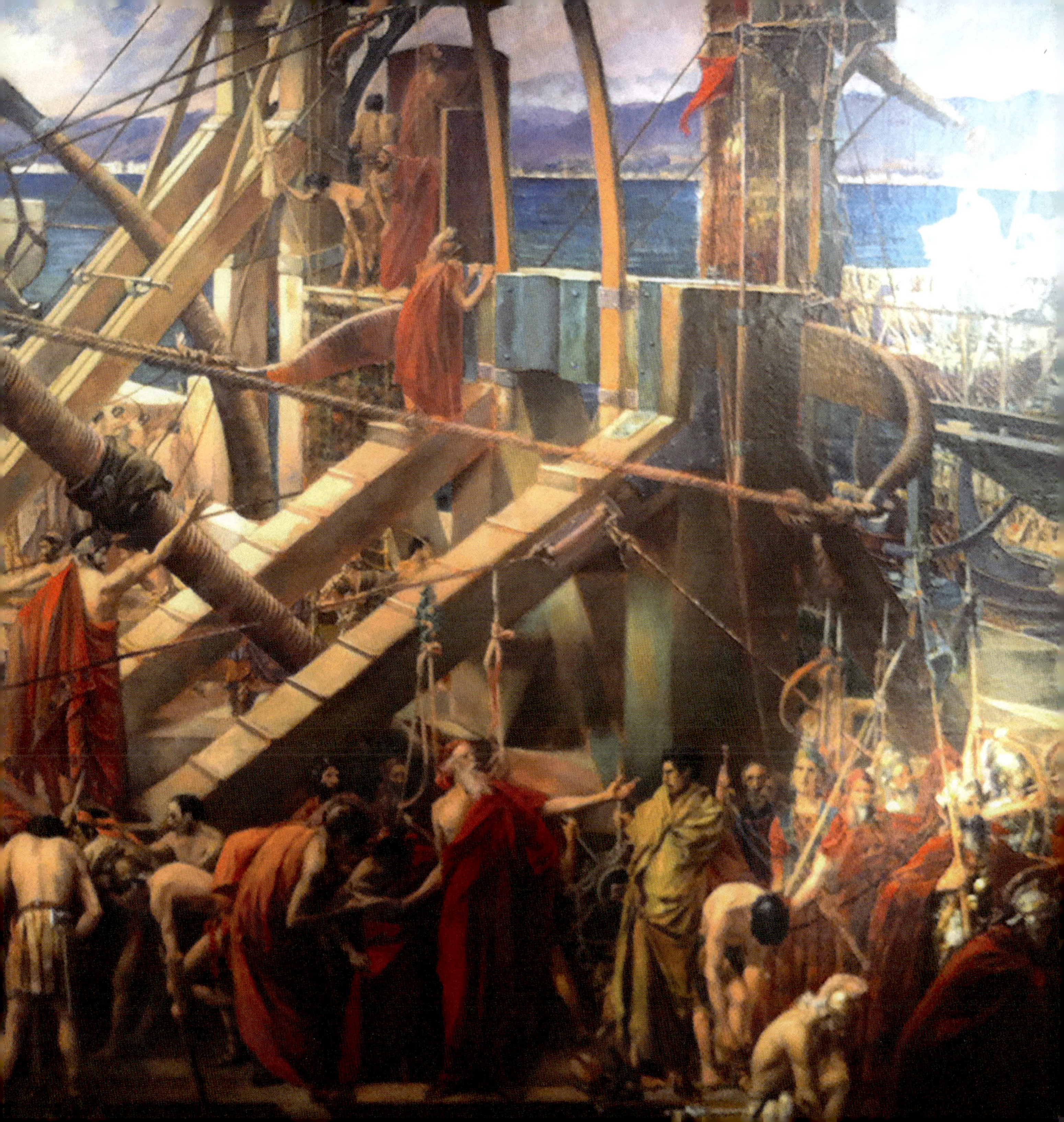

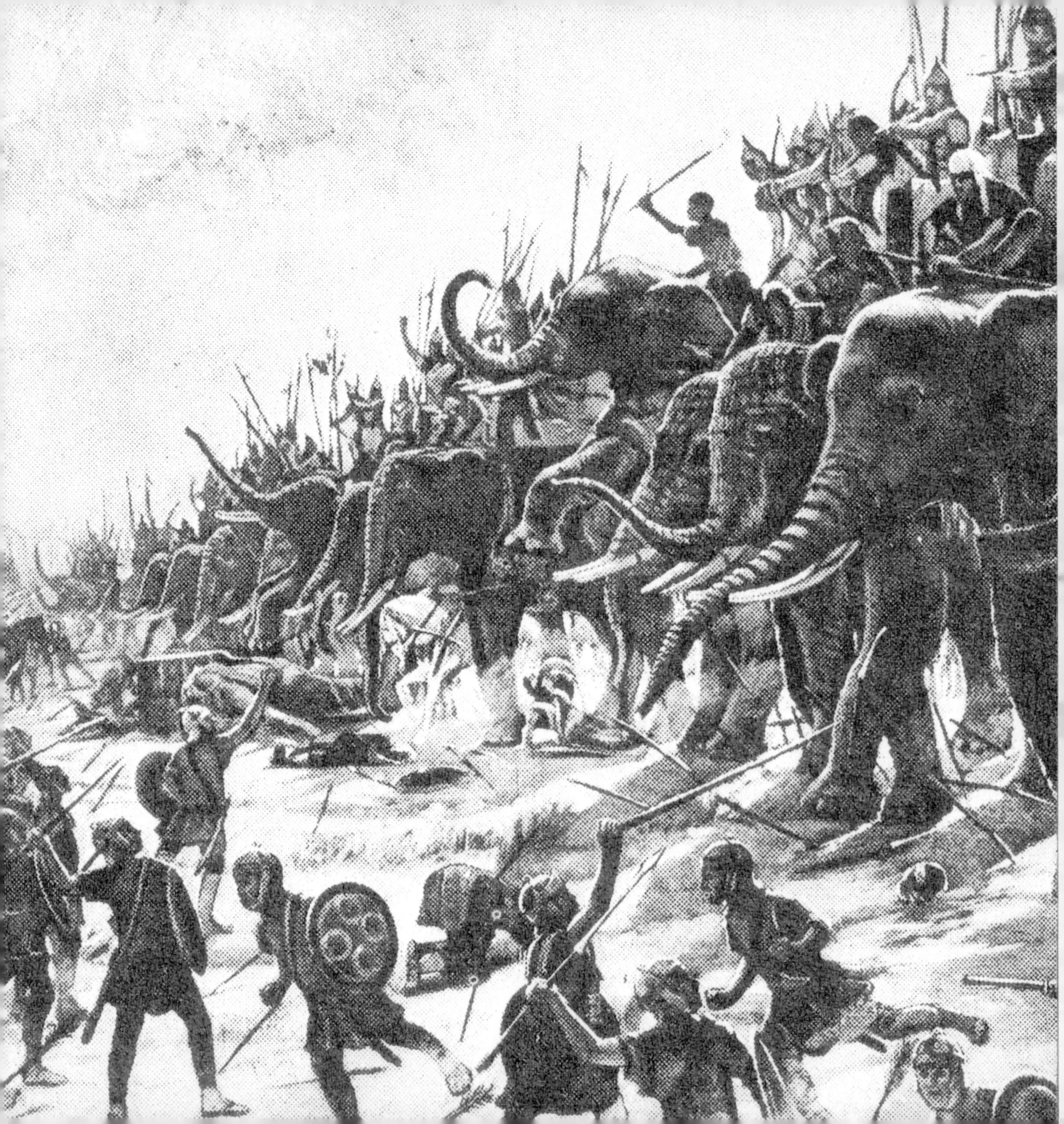

Battle of the Metaurus (207 B.C.E.)

Rome fought a series of wars with Carthage, often against the great general Hannibal. Hannibal was waiting for more troops and supplies his general Hasdrubal was bringing from Spain. The Roman forces trapped and defeated Hadrubal at the Metaurus river, preventing the two Carthaginian forces from linking up.

Battle of Pydna (168 B.C.E.)

The Roman Republic fought against the Macedonian forces under King Perseus, a descendant of Alexander the Great. The Greeks had more troops than the Romans, but the Roman legions were better trained, had better tactics, and were able to adjust to changing situations better. The Macedonians still mainly used the "phalanx", a dense mass of soldier with spears, and the legions were able to out-maneuver and outfight the phalanx formation. With this battle the Roman Republic extended its dominance over mainland Greece.

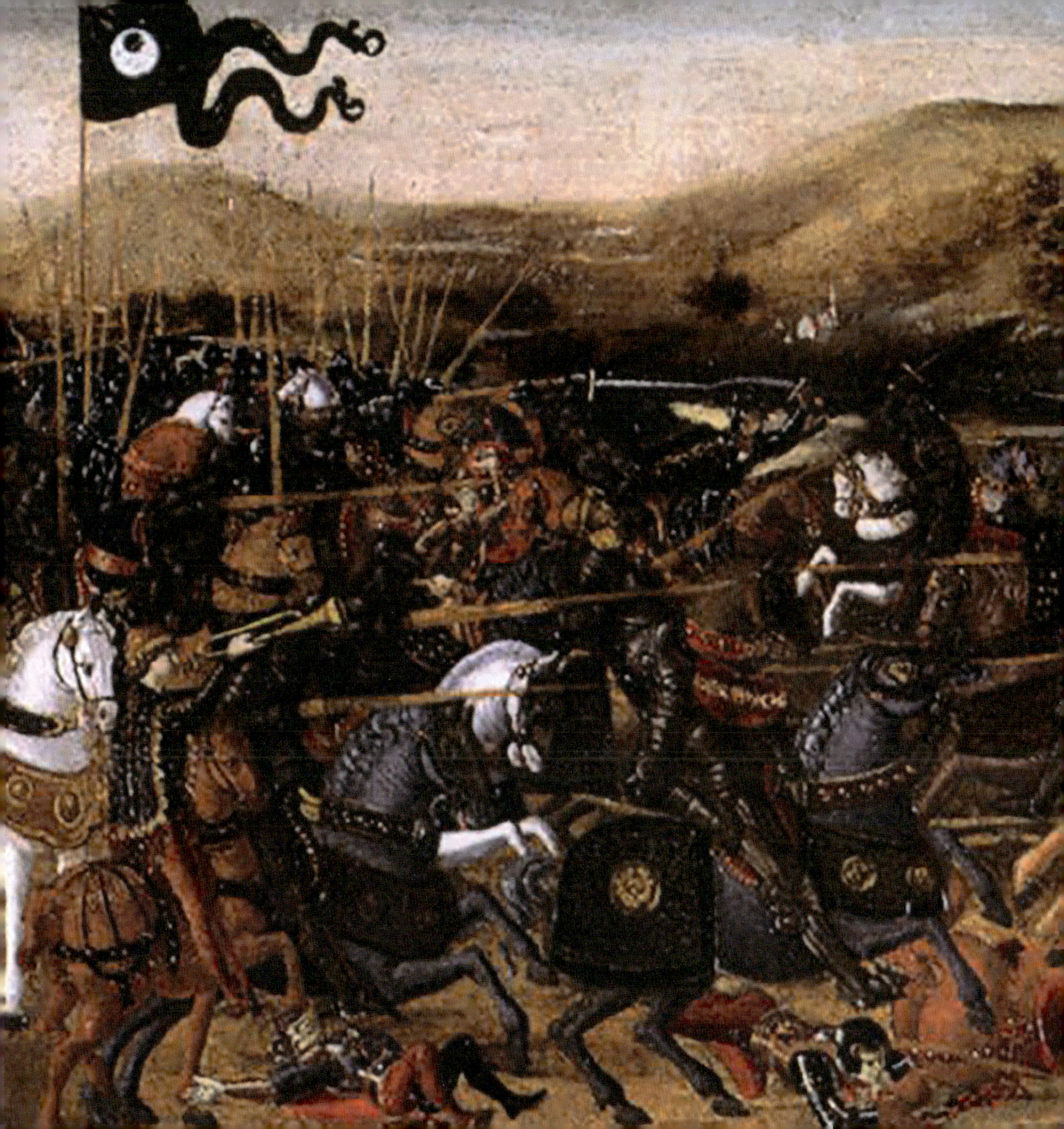

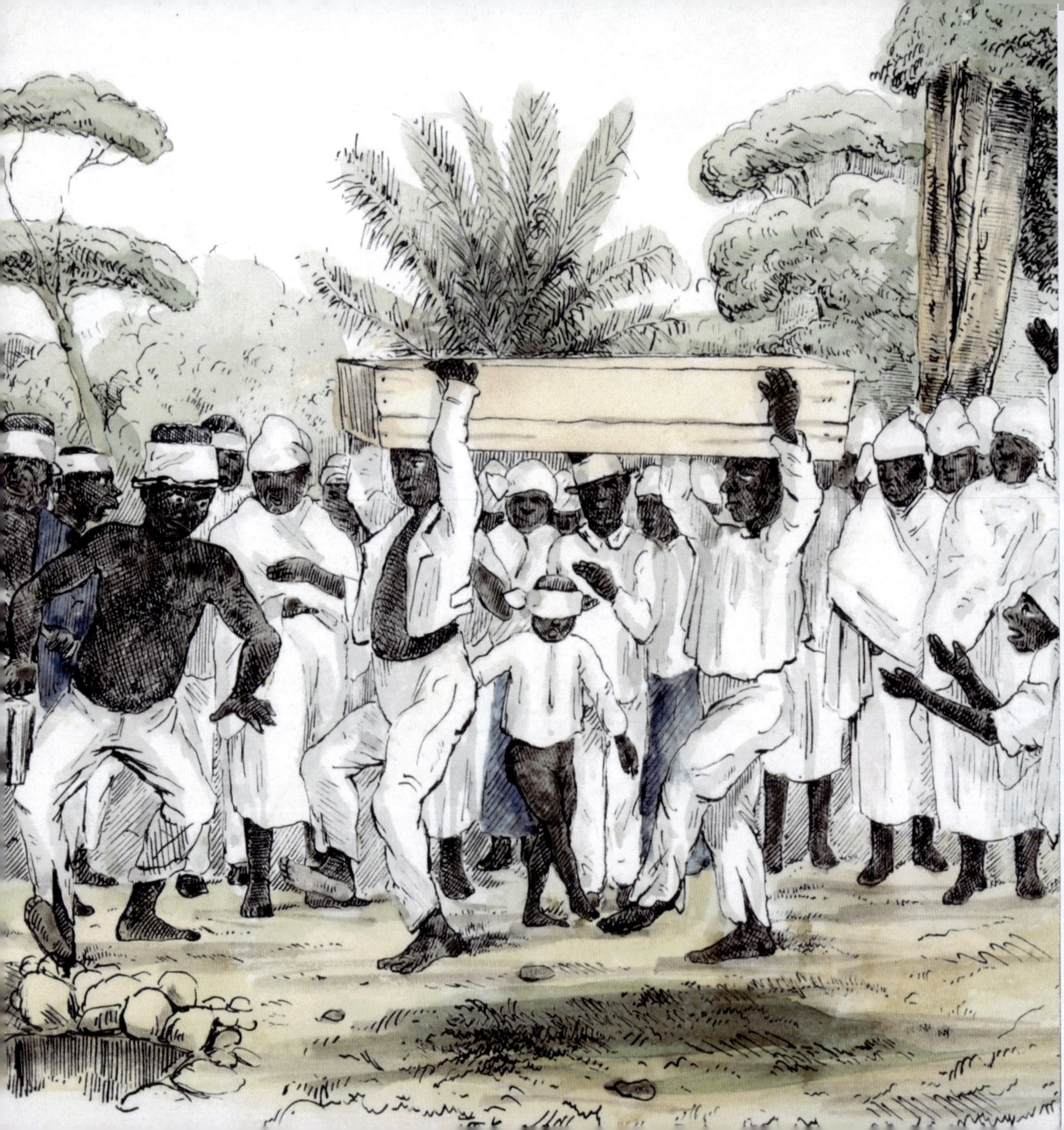

Third Servile War (73-71 B.C.E.)

For several decades Rome had to deal with slave rebellions, both by untrained slaves who worked the farms and other properties of Romans, and by the trained fighters who fought as gladiators in the arena for the amusement of the population. Most of these rebellions were small and short-lived.

However, under a gladiator named Spartacus, a rebellion grew until tens of thousands of slaves were in arms, and sometimes able to defeat the Roman legions that came out against them. The slaves controlled hill country to the south of Rome, and sometimes controlled towns and cities.

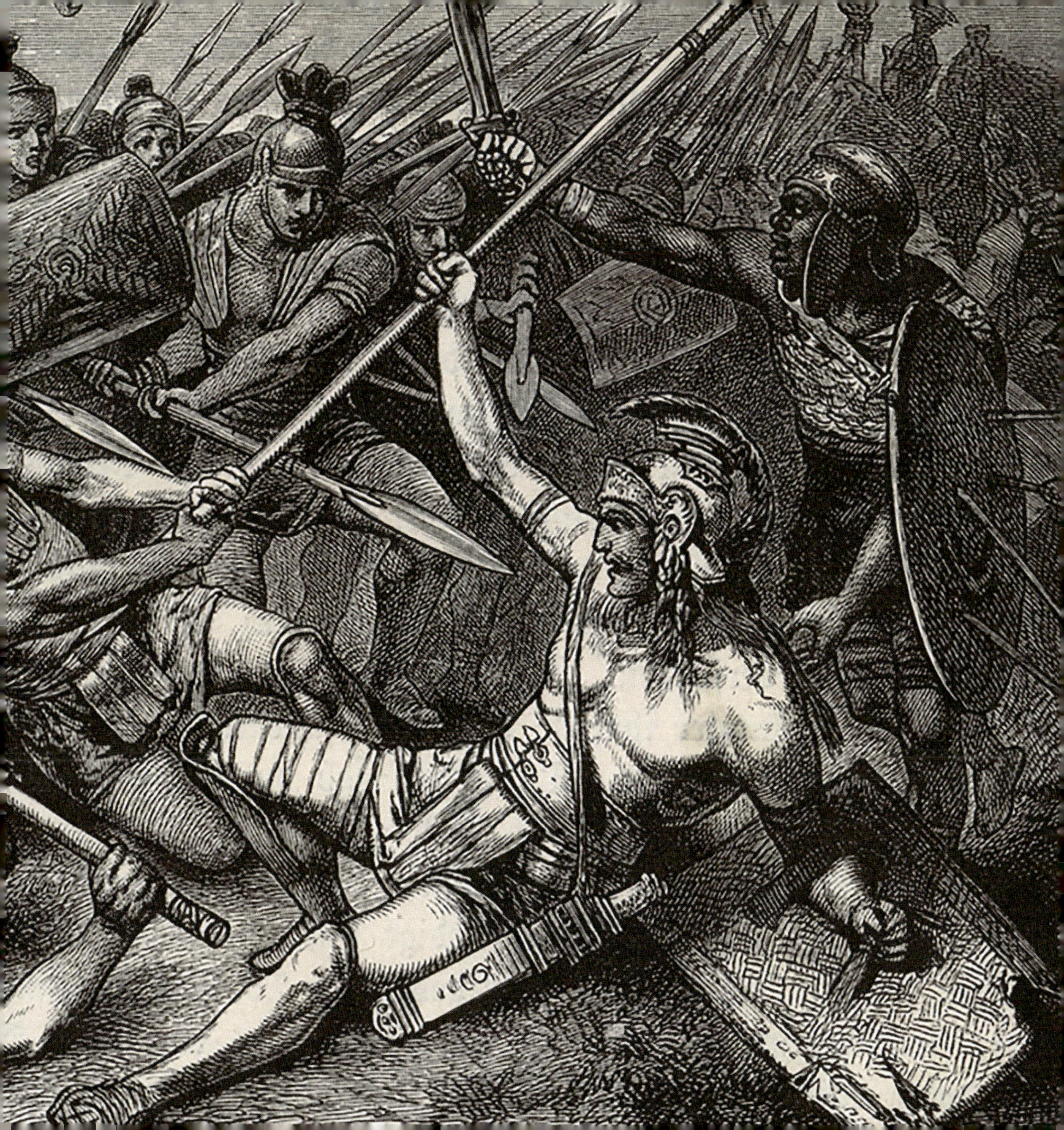

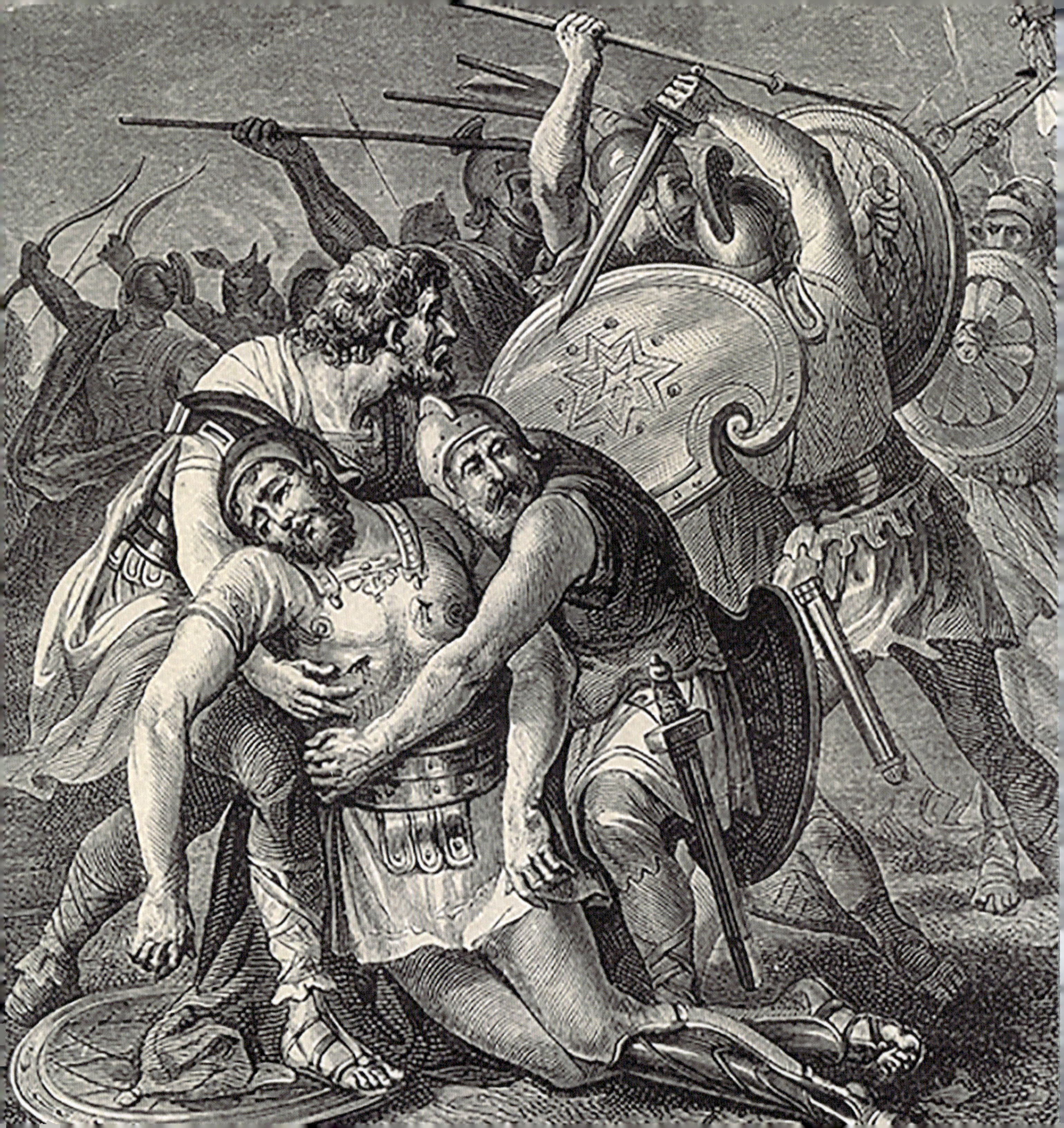

Generals Pompey and Crassus finally crushed the revolt during battles from 73 to 71 B.C.E. This raised the two generals to super-heroes in the eyes of the people, and they gained immense power in the Republic.

Battle of Carrhae (53 B.C.E.)

At Carrhae, in what is now Turkey, a huge Parthian army faced Roman legions under General Crassus. The Parthians heavy cavalry was better equipped and had better armor than did the Romans, and routed the Roman cavalry. The legions were defeated and the Parthians captured several legionary standards, or eagles.

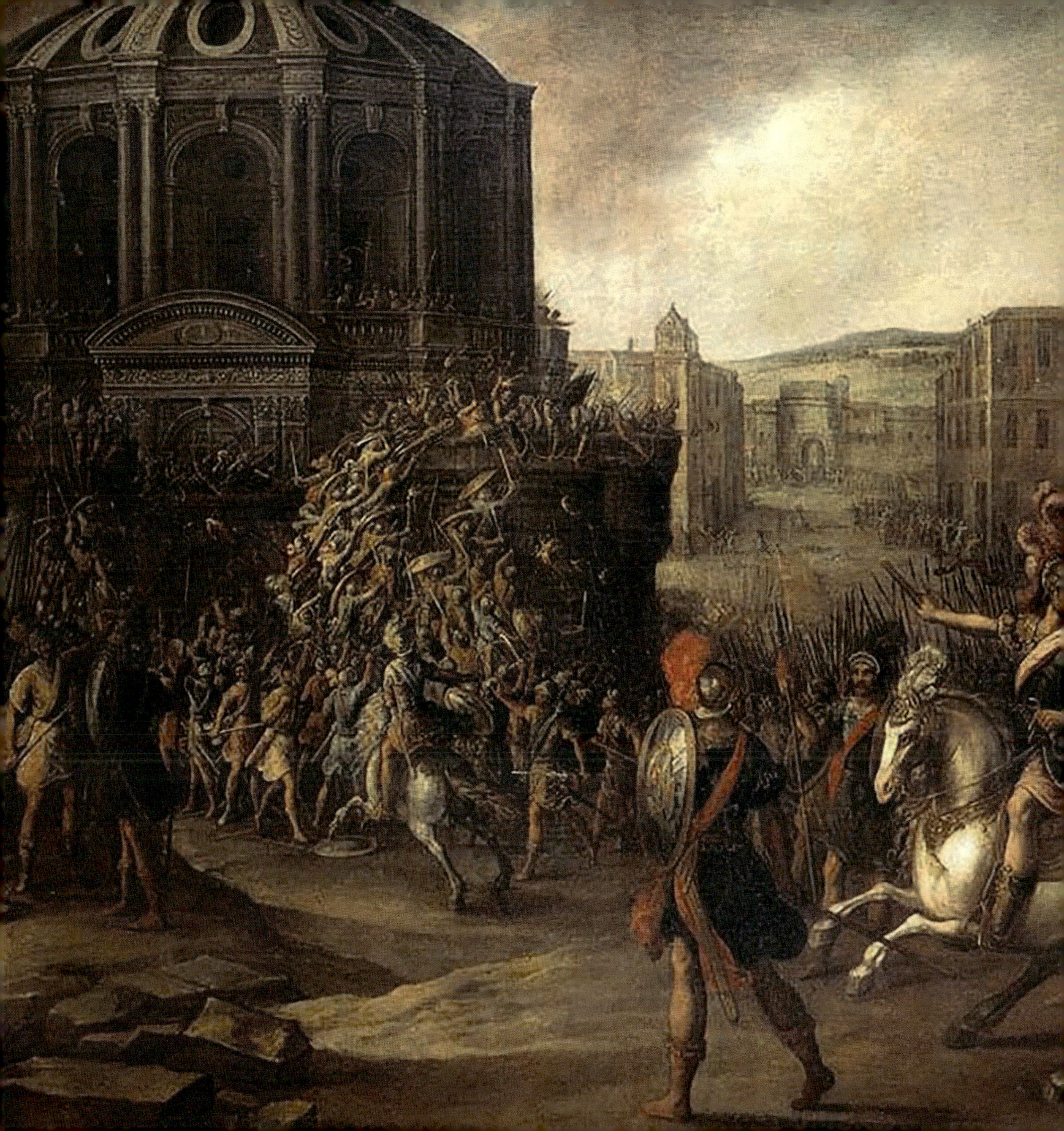

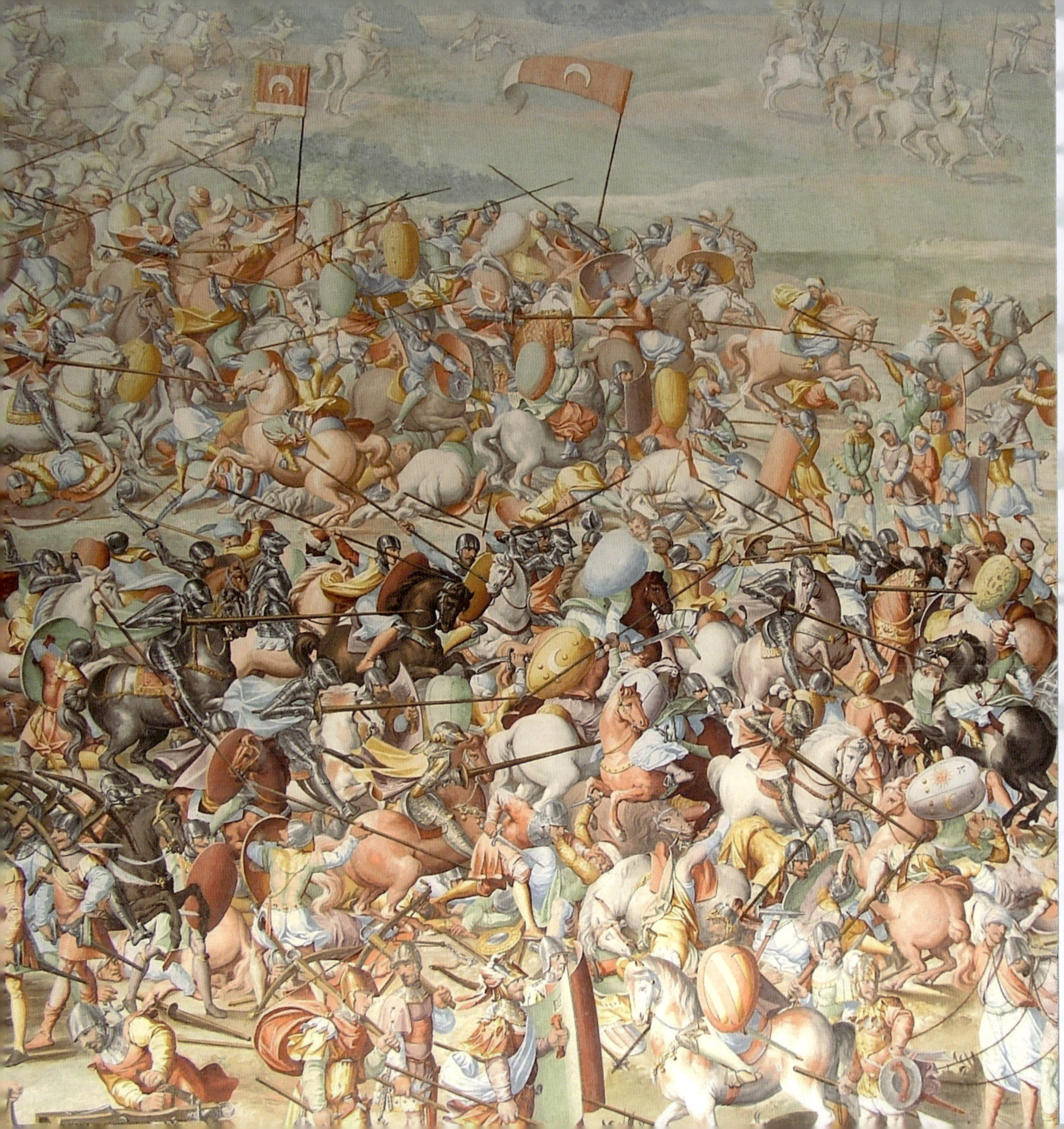

This was a devastating defeat for the Romans and indirectly led toward the end of the Republic and the rise of the Empire. People like Pompey argued that Rome needed a single strong man to prevent future disasters like Carrhae. An indirect benefit of this battle and the truce that followed it was that a fabric new to Romans, silk, began to be available to them through trade with Parthia.

Siege of Alesia (52 B.C.E.)

Julius Caesar was a great and energetic general. With his legions he conquered Gaul, what is now France, and led the first Roman incursion into Britain. He also defeated and neutralized Germanic tribes in what are now Belgium and Germany.

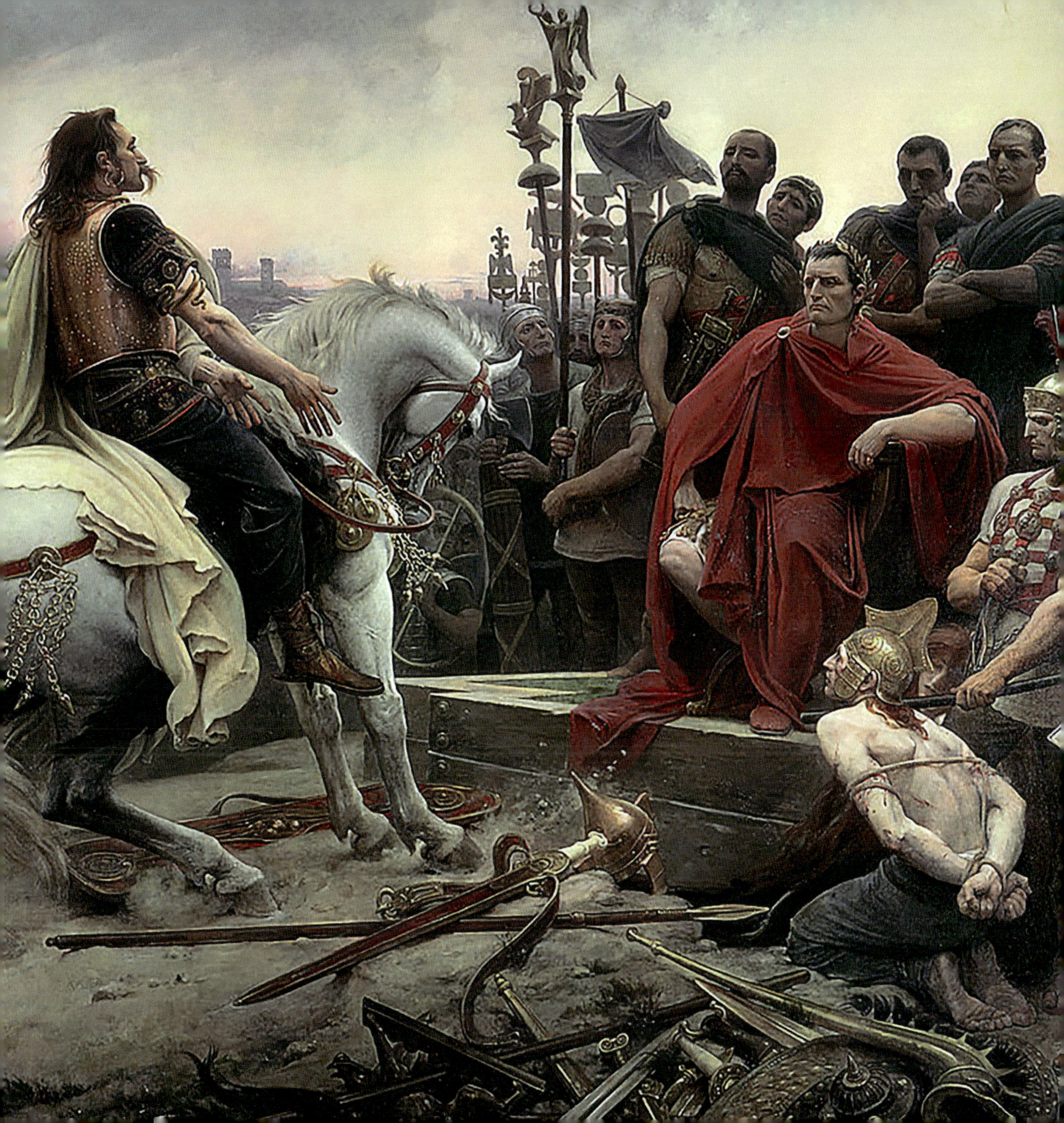

Julius Caesar

In France, the Gauls under Vercingetorix tried to defeat the Romans. Caesar forced them to retreat to their fortress at Alesia. The Gauls had more troops than the Romans, so Caesar knew he could not attack directly. He built walls and ditches around the whole fort, cutting it off from supplies and reinforcements.

The Gauls sent a relief force, and before it arrived the Romans built an outward-facing set of walls and ditches, so they were basically in a skinny, O-shaped fortification with Gauls both inside and outside the O.

Julius Caesar Forum and Temple of Venus

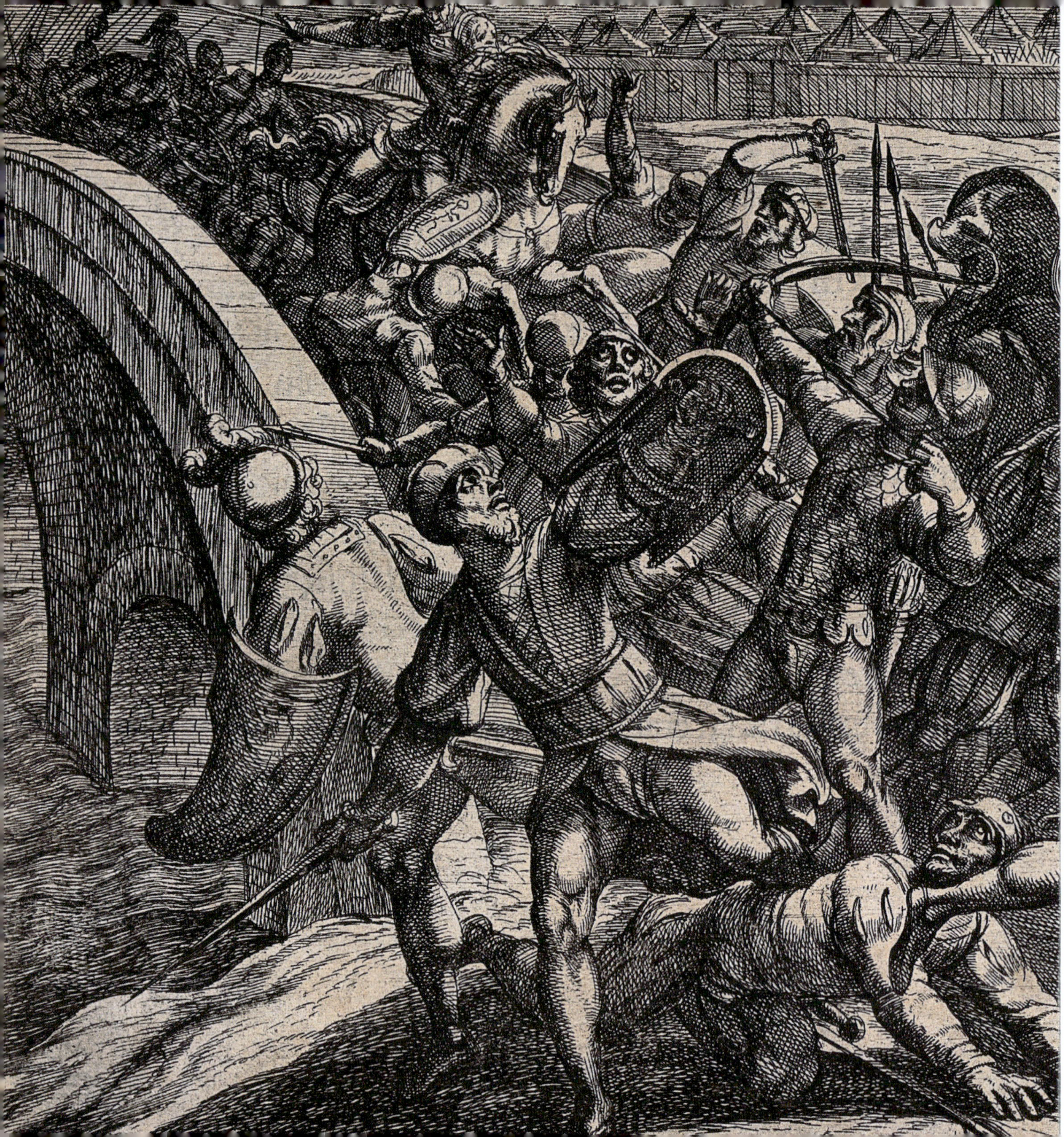

The Gauls inside the fort were starving, and when they tried to attack the Romans they could not fight their way through. The Gallic relief force broke through the Roman lines, but Caesar's cavalry defeated it. This victory secured Rome's control over Gaul and Caesar's rise as both a military and a political force in the Republic.

Battle of Pharsalus (48 B.C.E.)

Pompey and Julius Caesar were rivals for power in Rome. Their armies clashed in Greece, with Pompey's forces vastly outnumbering those of Caesar.

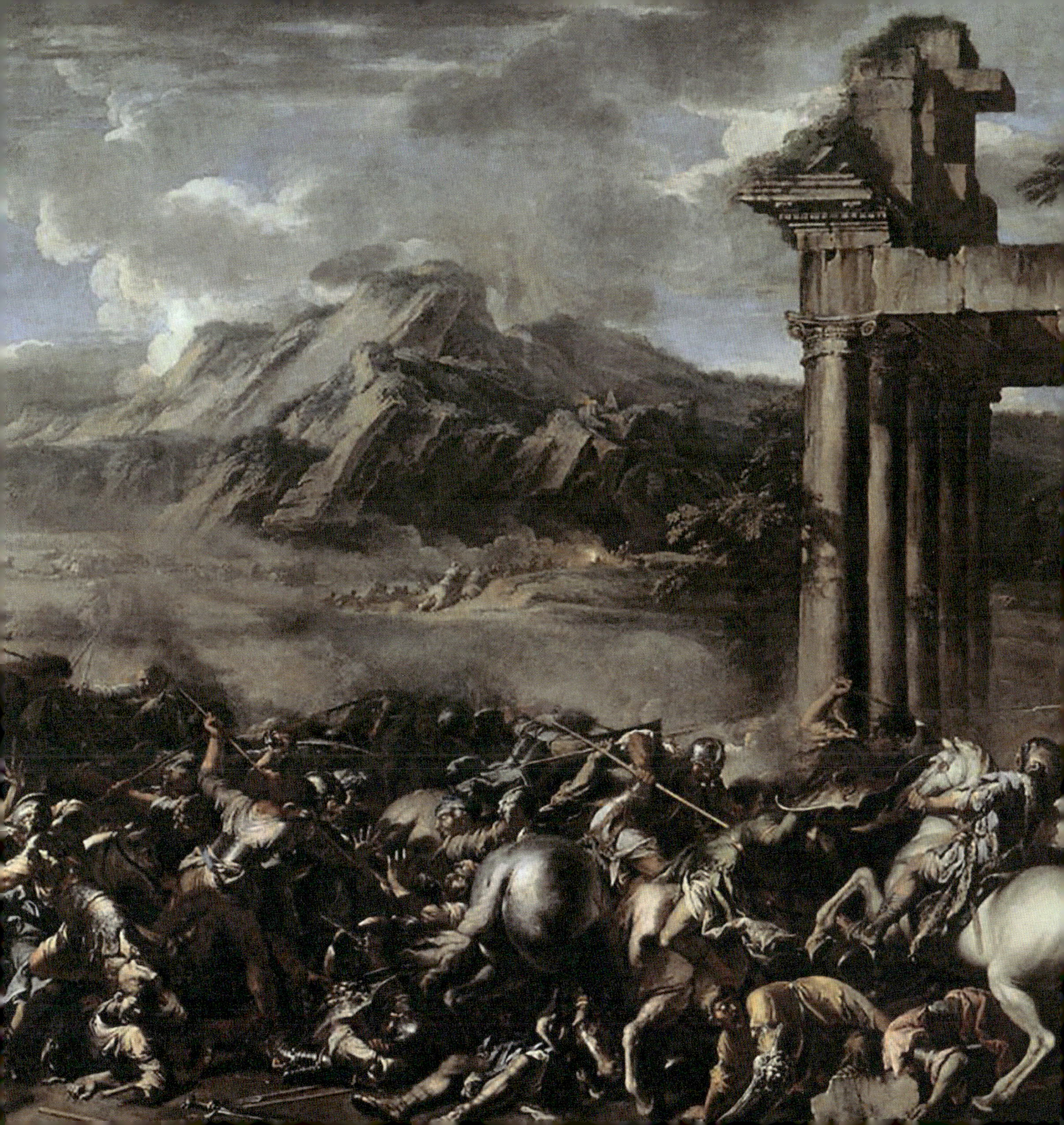

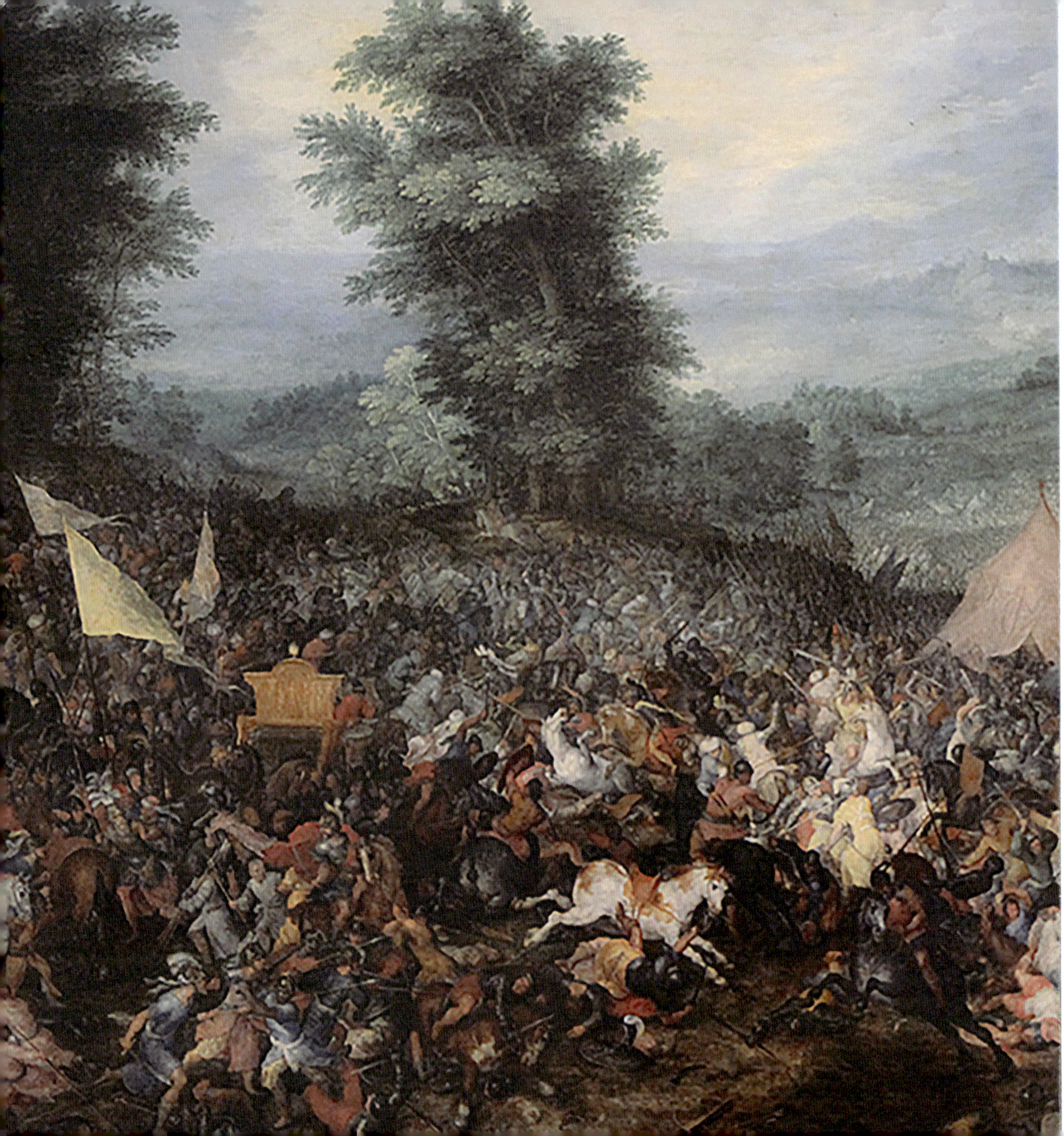

The armies faced each other with a river forming a barrier to one side of the battlefield. Caesar knew that Pompey had larger cavalry forces than his, and that if they could get by the other flank of his legions, they could attack him from the flank and rear. He hid units of spear-throwers on his exposed flank. When Pompey's cavalry made their attack, the spear-throwers surprised them, killed many horses and men, and send the cavalry into a panicked retreat. The panic spread to the rest of Pompey's army, and Pompey himself left the battlefield and eventually fled to Egypt.

Caesar had many more battles before he managed to defeat all of Pompey's forces, but Pharsalus was his key victory. He became the unquestioned leader of the Roman Republic.

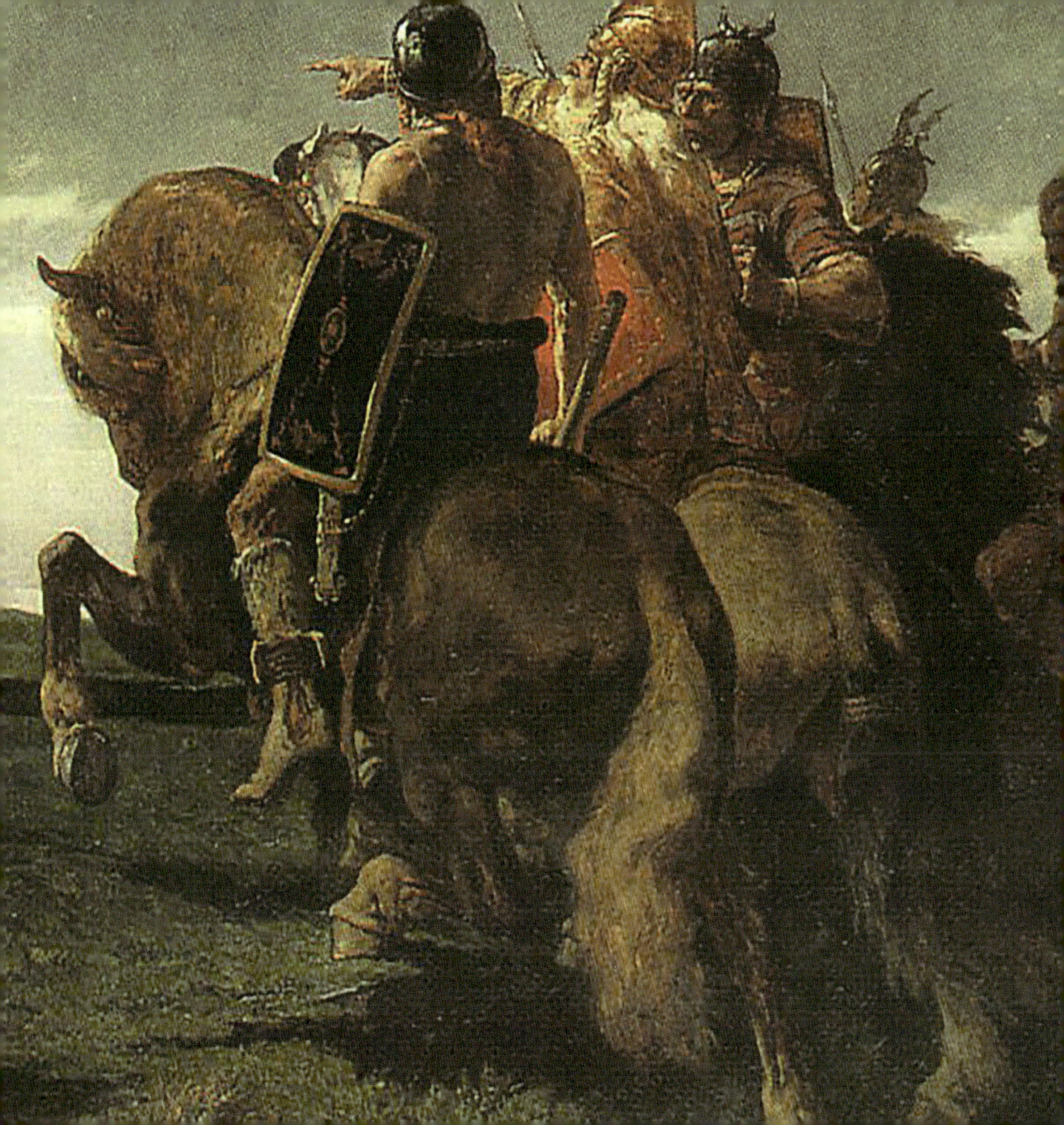

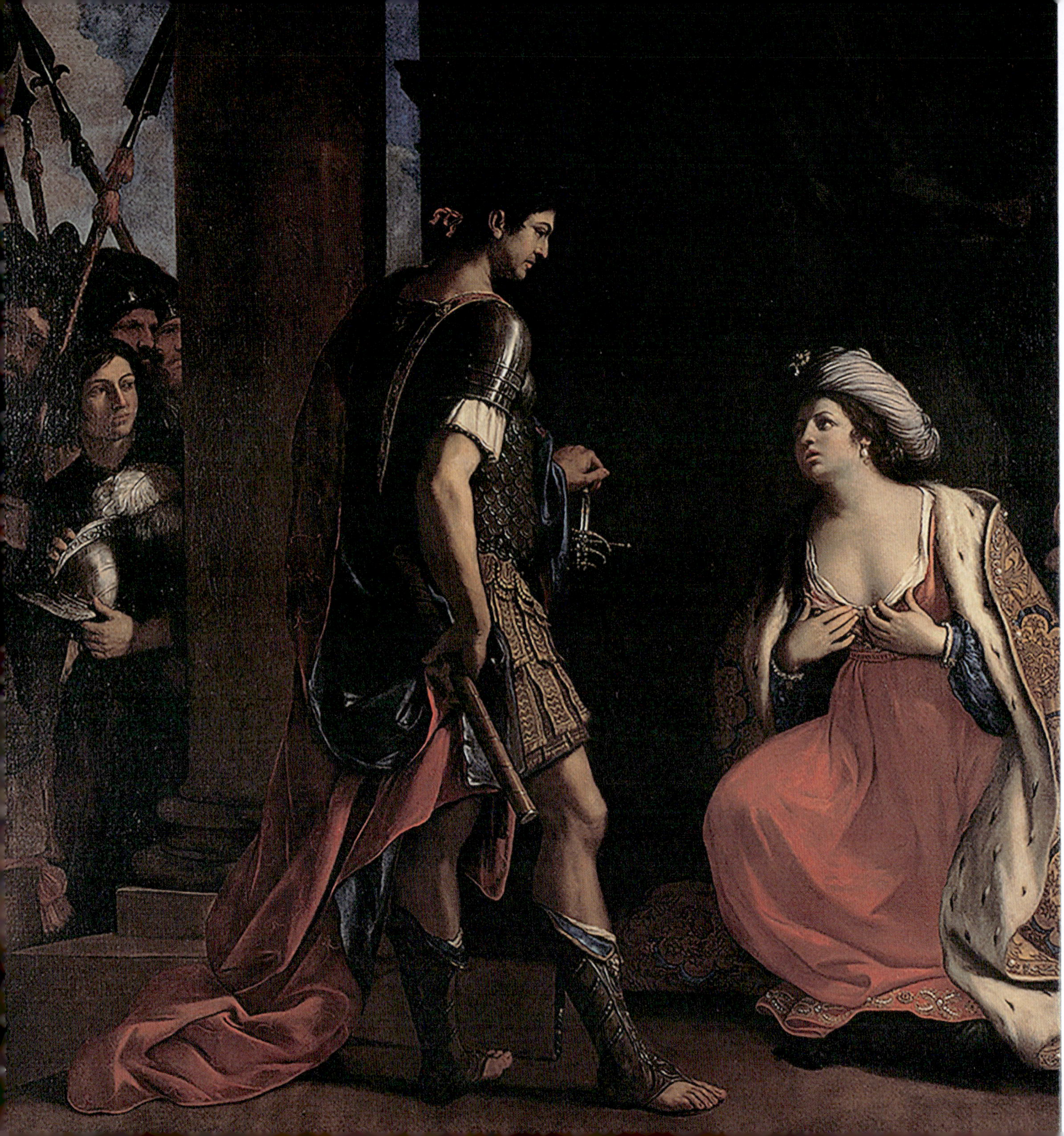

Caesar's enemies, fearful of his increasing power, assassinated him in the Senate building in Rome in 44 B.C.E. This led to further Roman-against-Roman wars out of which Octavian, who became Augustus, emerged as the victor and the first Emperor of Rome.

Battle of Actium (31 B.C.E.)

The Battle of Actium pitted Roman fleets against each other. On one side were the forces of Octavian, the adopted son of Julius Caesar who became Augustus, the first Emperor of Rome. On the other side were the Roman fleets under General Mark Antony and the Egyptian navy lead by Cleopatra.

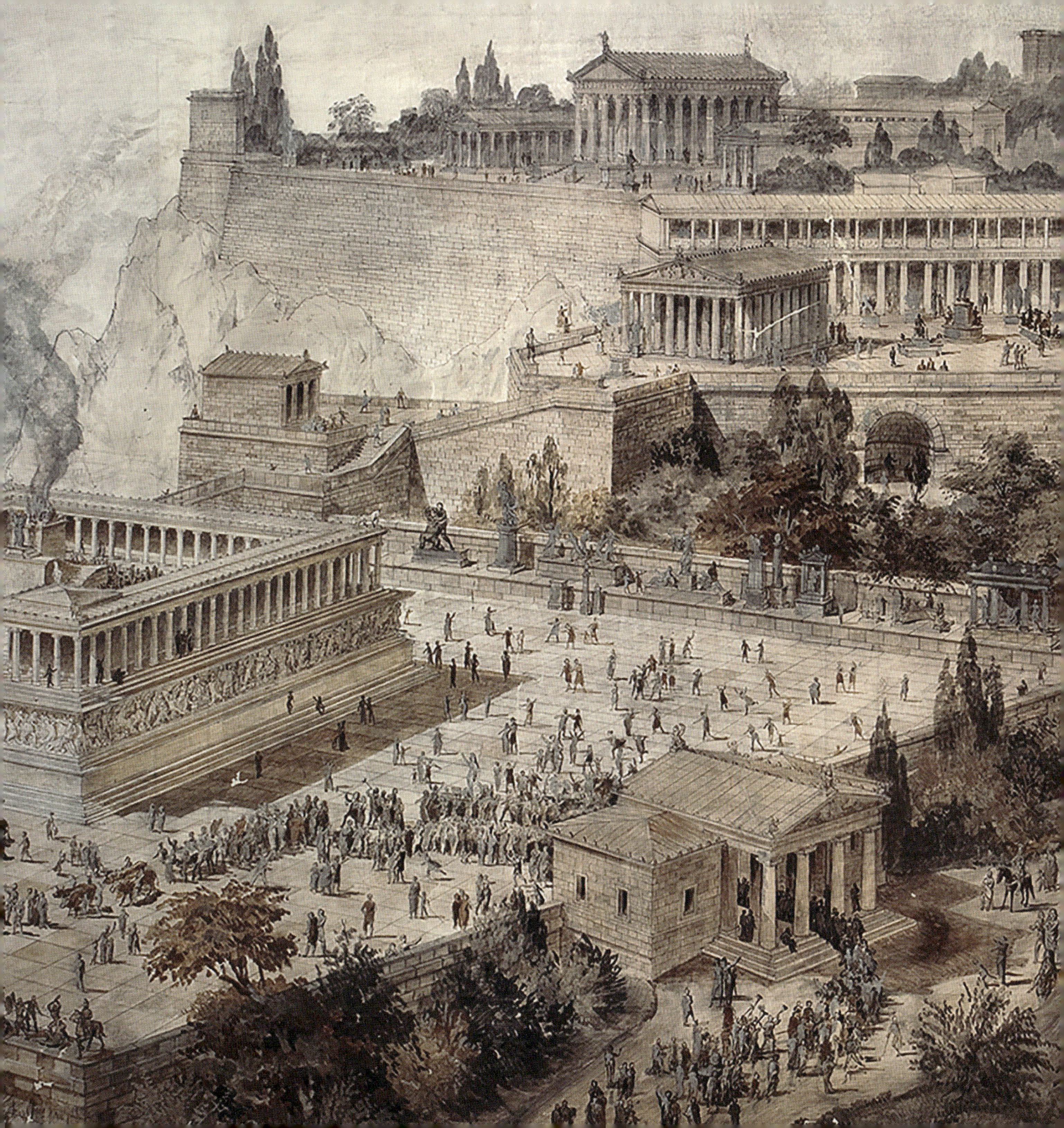

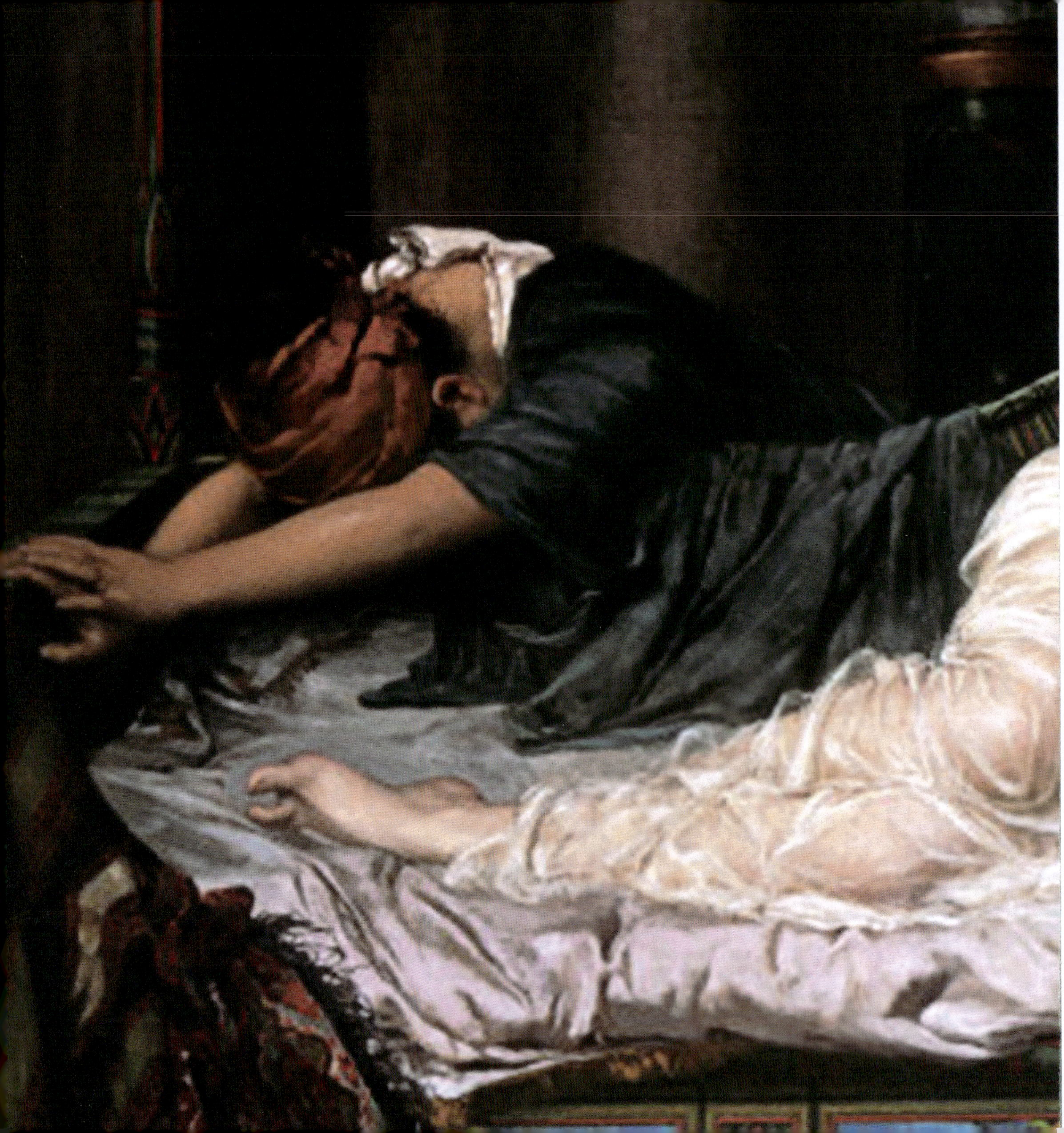

Octavian's forces won the battle and consolidated his power over the Republic/Empire. Forces that had been loyal to Mark Antony began to desert his side. Thinking that Cleopatra had been killed, Mark Antony killed himself. When Cleopatra heard this news she also killed herself.

Octavian's victory cleared away the rivals to his taking power in Rome. Although he still talked about the Roman Republic, he accepted titles and honors that were the beginning of the style and actions of the Roman emperors.

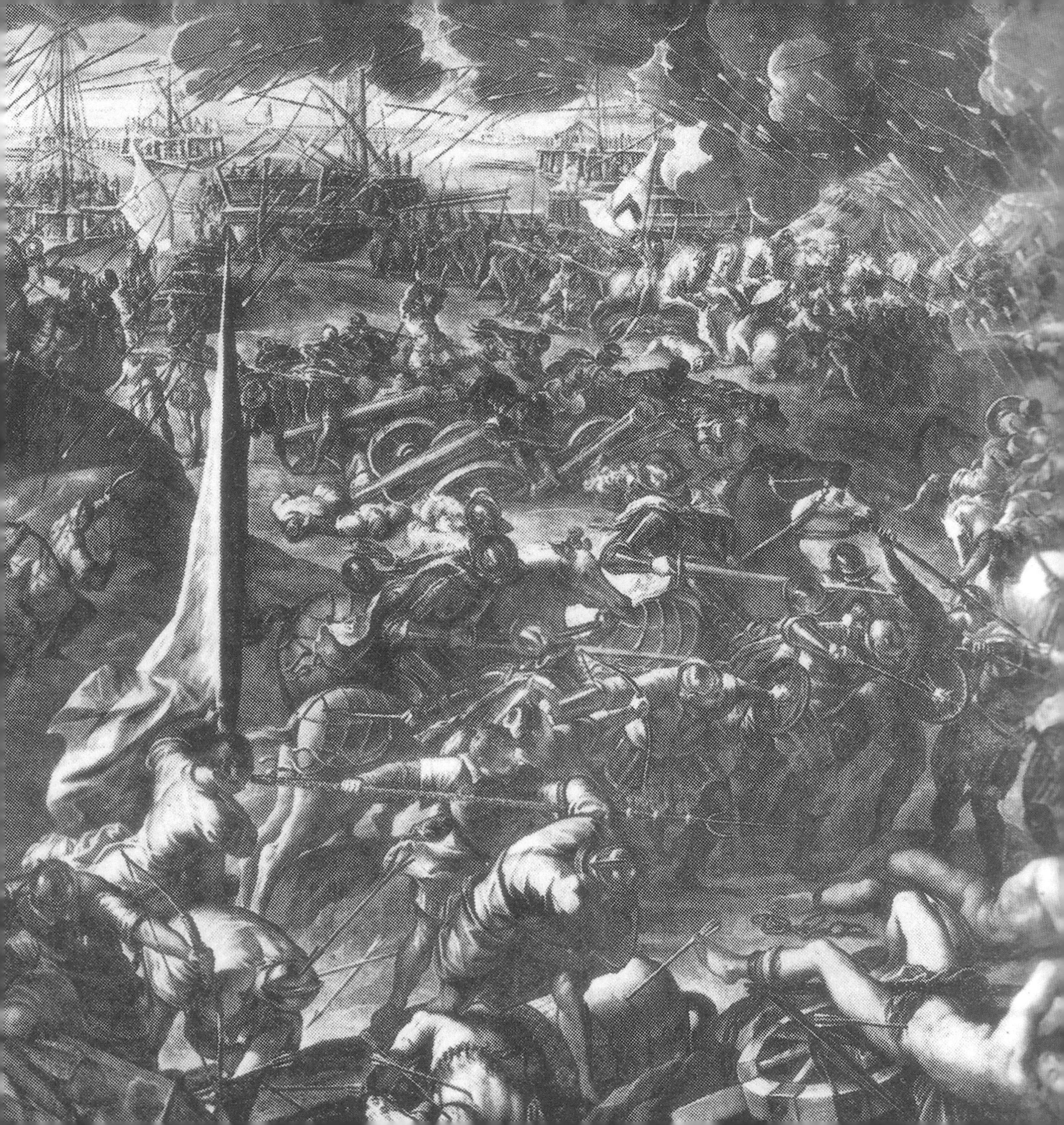

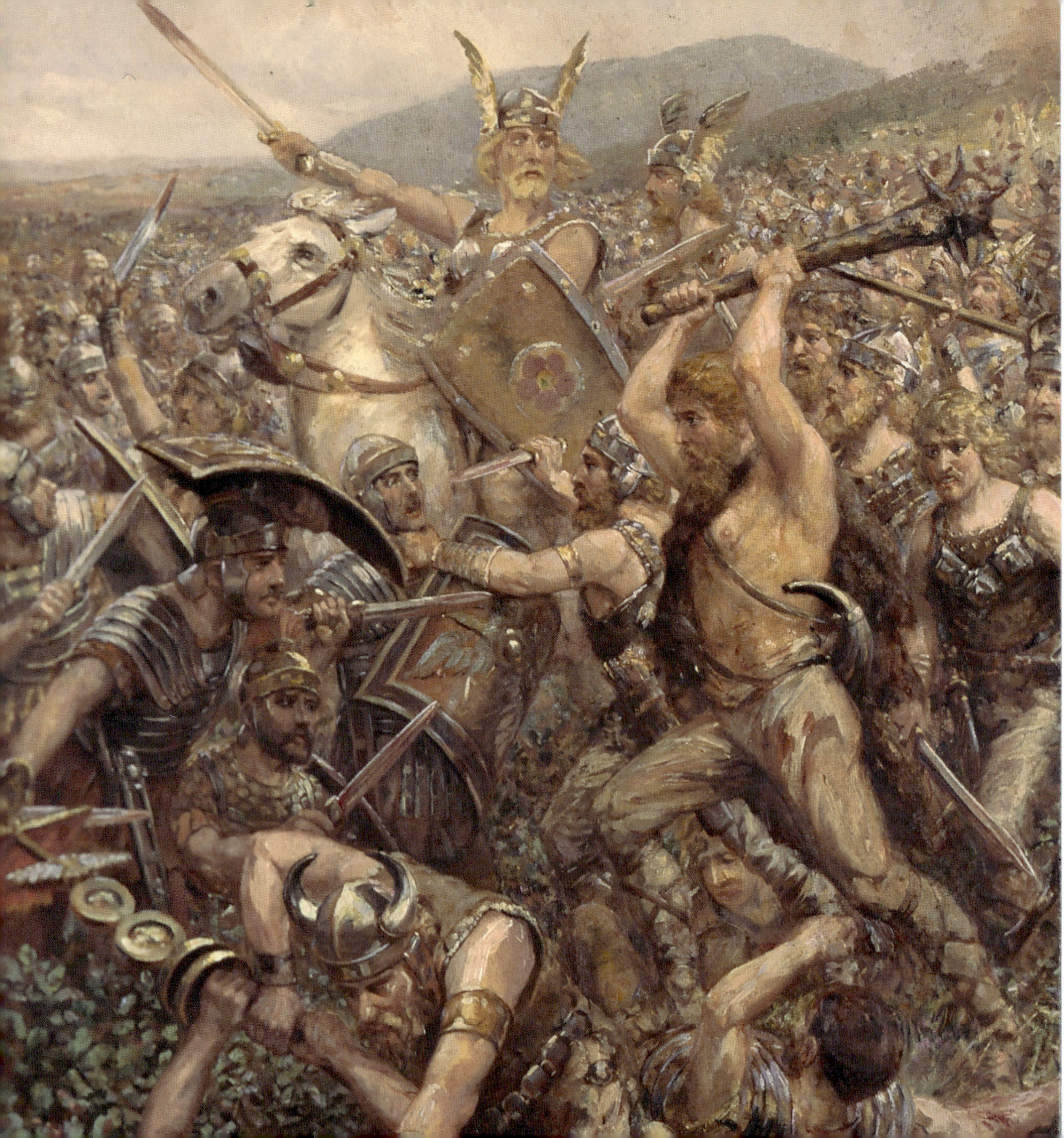

Battle of the Teutoburg Forest (9 C.E.)

The young Roman Empire expanded its territory east and north. In the north the legions pushed into Germanic territory, fighting tribes they called "barbarians."

At the Teutoburg Forest, north of the Rhine River, the tribal forces destroyed three Roman legions in a multi-day series of ambushes and guerrilla warfare until the remaining Roman troops could not repel a final mass attack. From this battle, Rome acknowledged that the Rhine River was effectively its northern frontier.

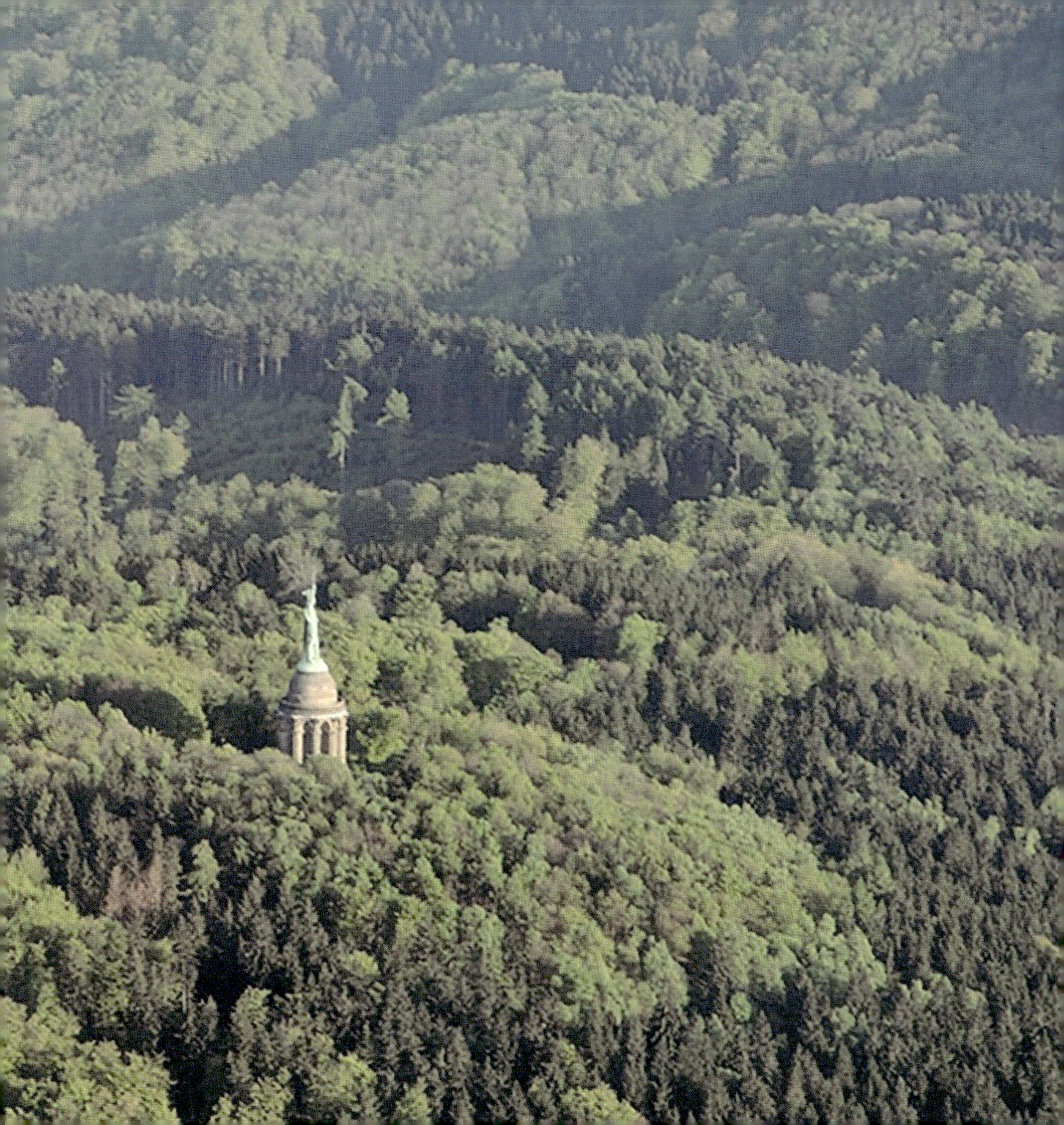

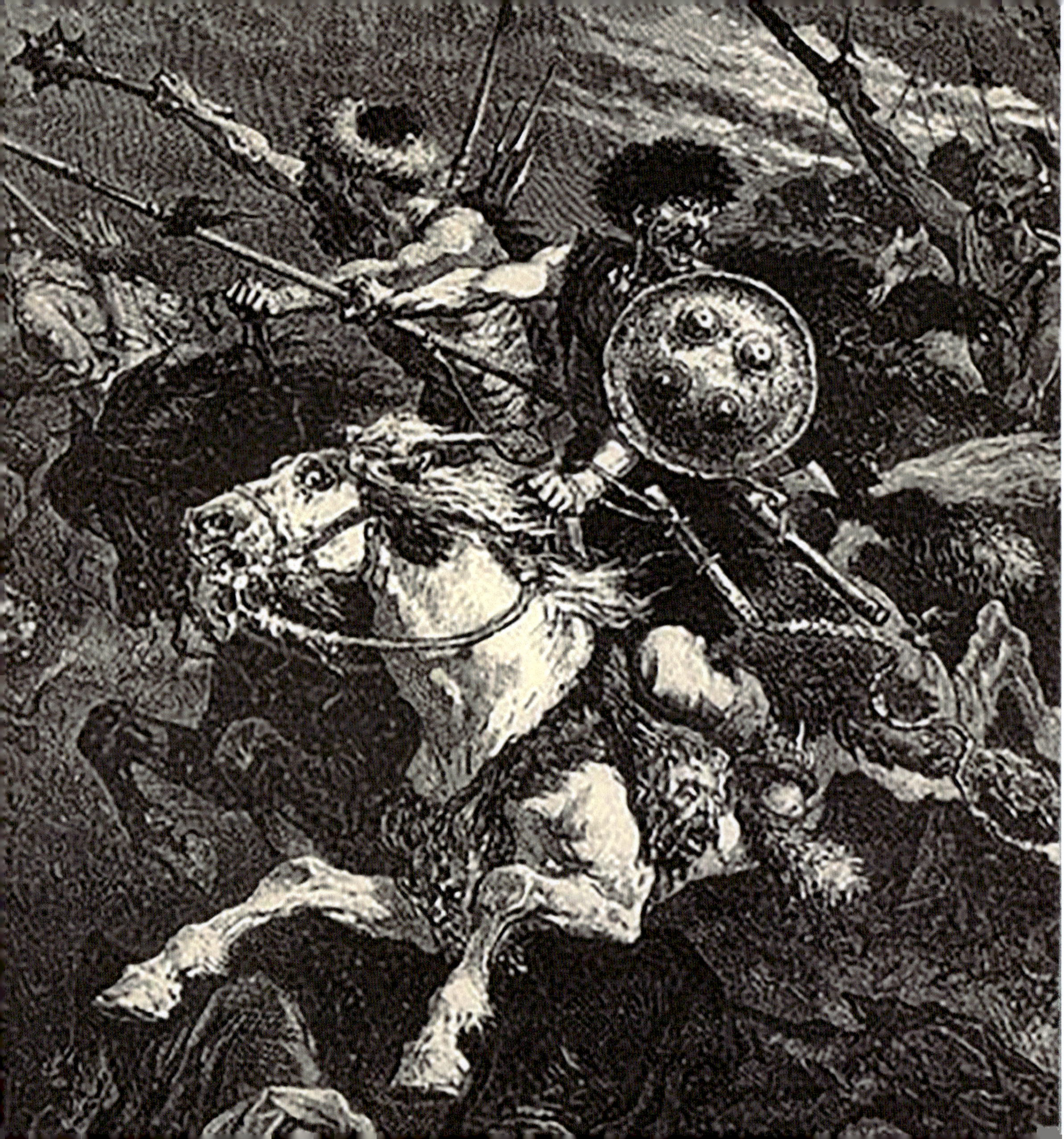

Battle of Châlons (274 C.E.)

Gauls in what is now France, rebelled against the Roman Empire and maintained an independent empire for 13 years. At Châlons the Roman armies soundly defeated the Gauls, destroying their army. This reunited the territories of Rome in Western Europe.

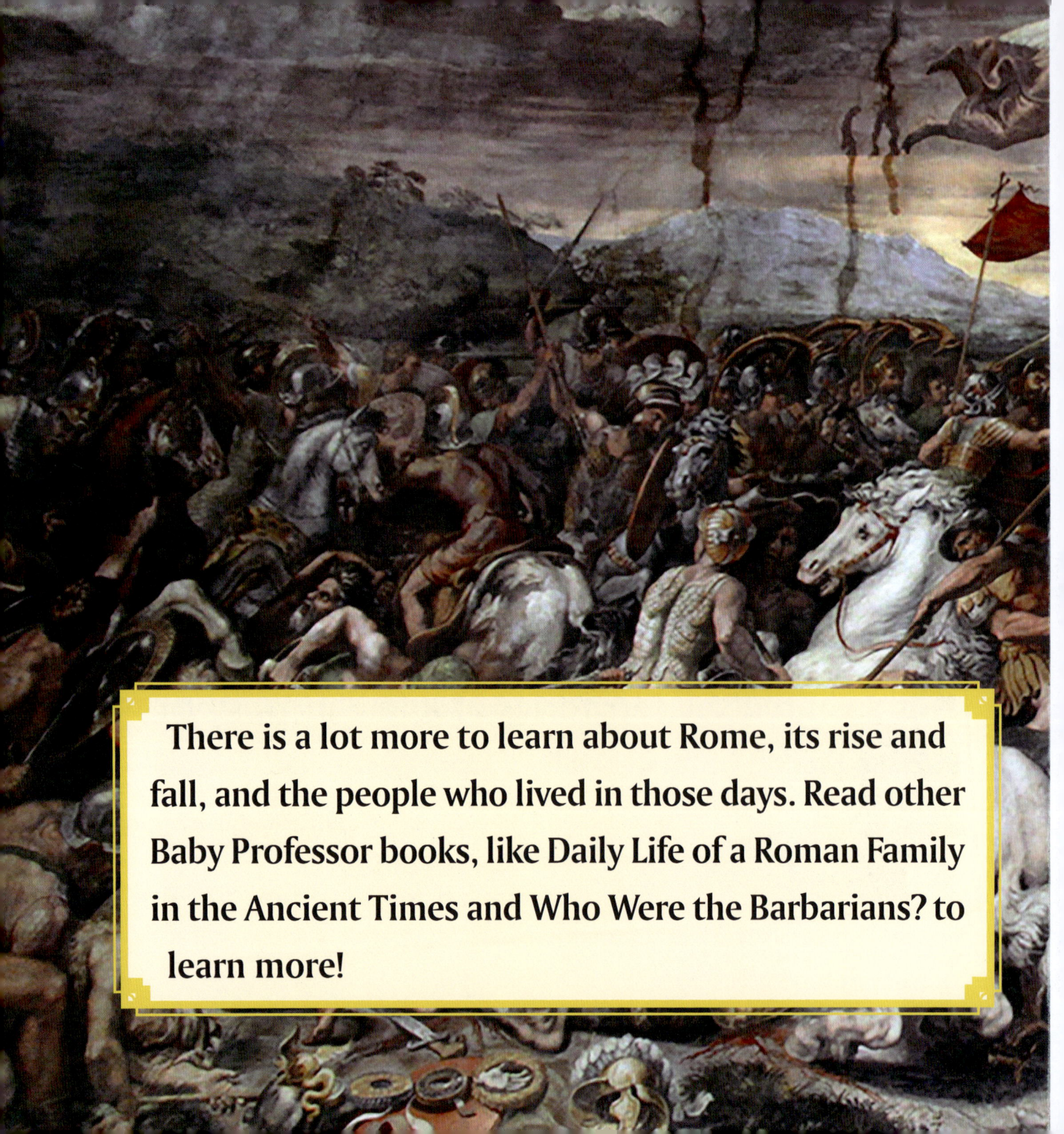

There is a lot more to learn about Rome, its rise and fall, and the people who lived in those days. Read other Baby Professor books, like Daily Life of a Roman Family in the Ancient Times and Who Were the Barbarians? to learn more!

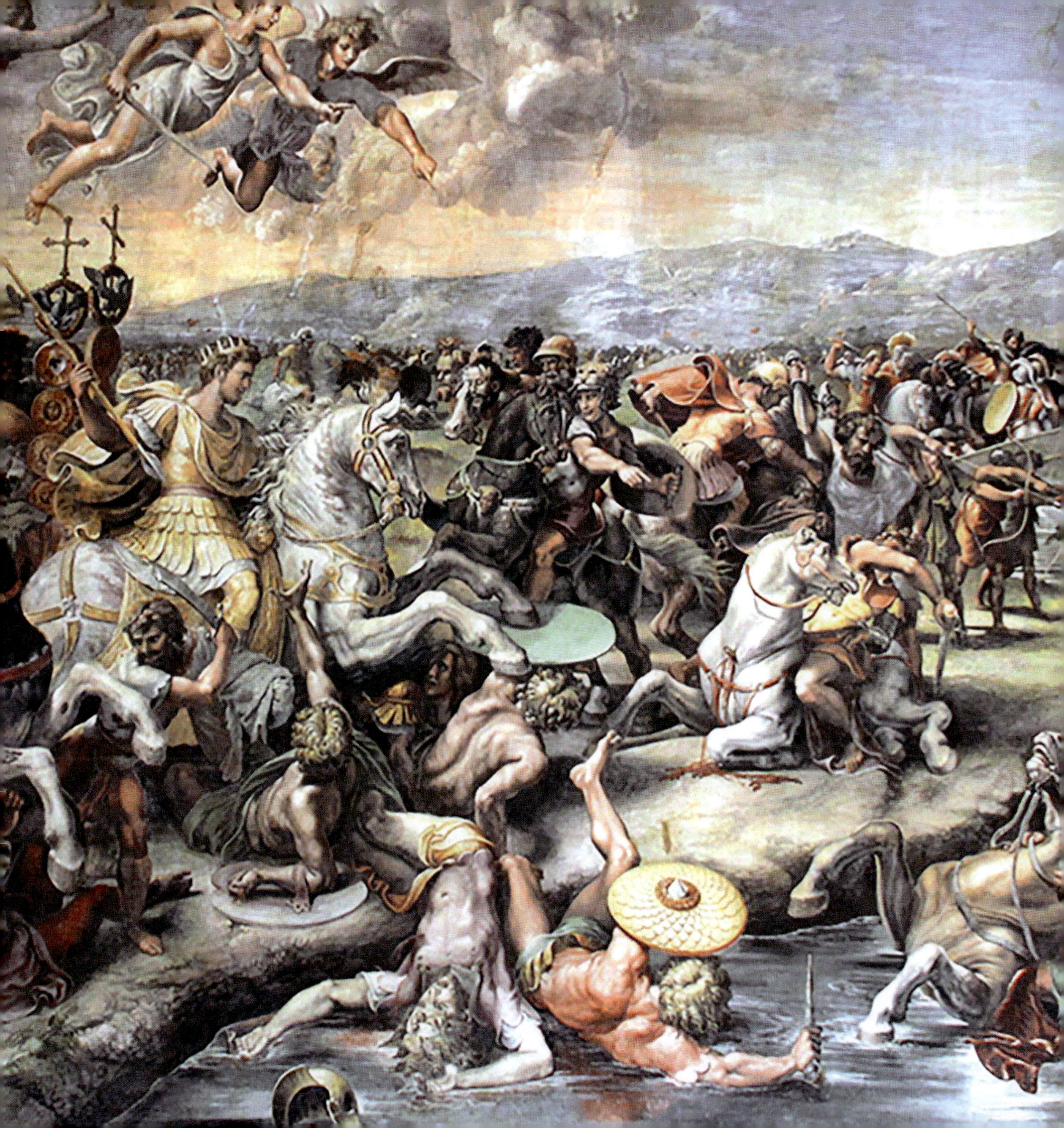

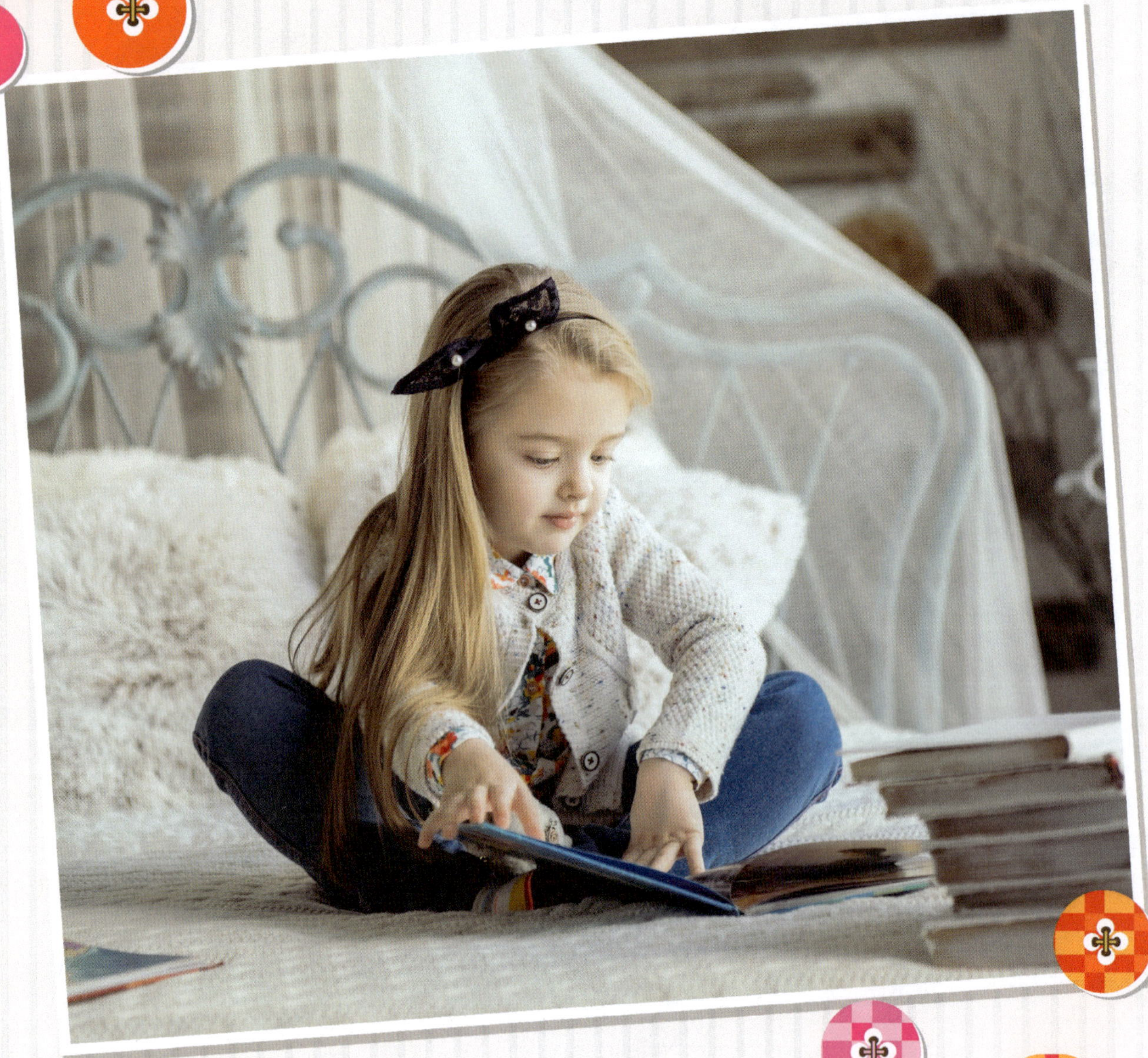

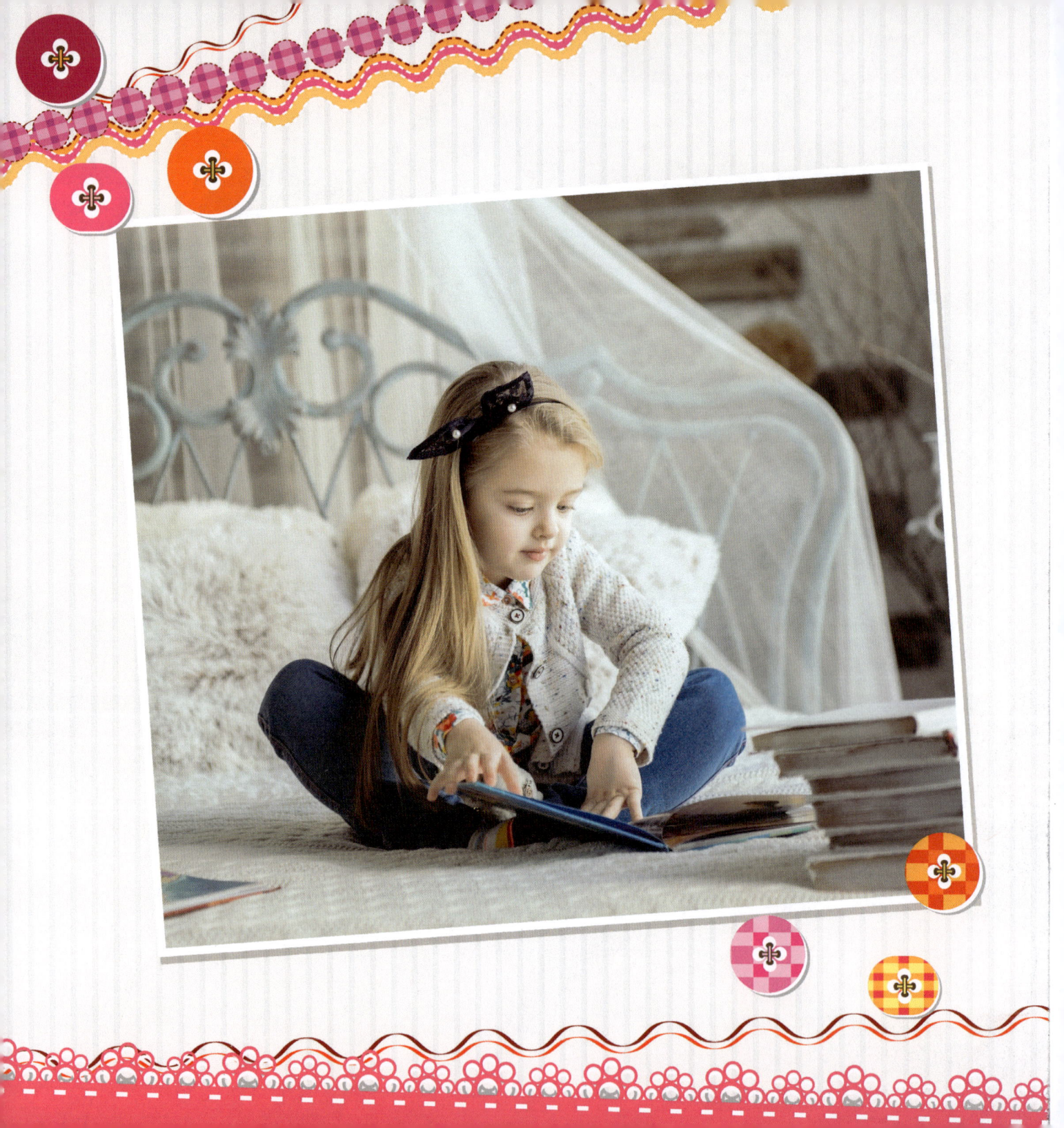

Visit

BABY PROFESSOR
EDUCATION KIDS

www.BabyProfessorBooks.com

to download Free Baby Professor eBooks and view our catalog of new and exciting Children's Books

Printed in Great Britain
by Amazon